An Angel with a Broken Wing

An Angel with a Broken Wing

Cleopatra Sorina Iliescu

MOUNTAIN ARBOR
PRESS
Alpharetta, GA

Copyright © 2017 by Cleopatra Sorina Iliescu

All rights reserved. No part of this book may be reproduced or transmitted in any form or by any means, electronic or mechanical, including photocopying, recording, or any information storage and retrieval system, without permission in writing from the author.

ISBN: 978-1-63183-111-9

10 9 8 7 6 5 4 3 2   0 6 2 2 1 7

Printed in the United States of America

∞This paper meets the requirements of ANSI/NISO Z39.48-1992 (Permanence of Paper)

*I dedicate my verses to the divine,
as through the divine I am inspired to write
about the divine beauty I see all around us.*

Contents

Acknowledgments	ix
Introduction	xi
Ready to Fly	1
A Nest	23
Water	45
Nihil	67
I Bow to All	89
In the Moment	111
The Symphony of Life	133
Tryptics	155
The Blissful Feminine	177
Dew	197
A New Page	219

Acknowledgments

There is not one single poem that belongs to me. They are the property of the village that stood by my side, encouraged me to grow into my own shoes, and supported me to manifest fully and freely in all my artistic expression. Dreams were born to me. The talent to write was a gift from the heavens. However, it is the fondness and appreciation of the people to whom I am dear and who are dear to me, that brought me the strength to persevere, propped me up every time I fell, and cheered for me all the way up to the finish line. I am always inspired, always playing with ideas, but my friends gave me the courage to push on. They are the ones who showed me the value and purpose of sharing my work with the world. The talent to write is a gift from heaven not for me to keep buried, but for me to bring forth for its light to shine warmly on other hearts, on other souls.

Ultimately, I bow my head, full of gratitude to God, for I did nothing to deserve neither talent nor goodhearted friends, nor the chance to fulfill the dreams that were born to me since before my birth.

Special thanks to my friends Ute Von Wietersheim, Daciana Dao, Alisa Abdulaeva, Natalya Myasinkova, Susan Ryan, Donna Labagh, Doli Bota, and Jody Lockamy for their encouragement and support. Thank you, with gratitude, to Mountain Arbor Press's team for working with me diligently to make my dream of publishing possible. Many thanks as well to the Kennesaw State University Writing Center for their additional help with proofreading my manuscript.

Introduction

I write not because of what I would aspire to become, but because of what I always was at heart: a poet. I write not because I have something to say, but because I have something to share: my heart. And my heart throbs, moved by the extraordinary beauty transparent through nature's every detail. I perceive patterns, and in all patterns I also see the uniqueness of new beginnings, of new possibilities impinging like sprouts upon fixed configurations to break free. I look at the world through empathy lenses, identifying both the greatness and the murkiness within each and any phenomenon not on a black-white continuum, but rather as a colorful rhizome that sends out roots and shoots as it spreads out in a regular irregularity.

I hang from clouds sometimes. Sometimes I watch the world from its side with my head tilted. I move forward, sideways, and backward, one and two, two and one, like a knight in a chess game. I am analyzing a situation, an event, an issue, a thought, a feeling from inside-out and outside-in and from the side of another. I consider different angles and points of reference, being aware that I cannot possibly know nor portray the truth in its wholeness. At the very least I could capture facets of it—little snapshots of reality that might hold true in a certain context, for a certain circumstance, at a certain time… And sometimes—really just sometimes—I see the same old, the old since the beginning of time, in a different light, in awe at the possibility that our whole universe might be so different than what we hold as known, as truth, as common-sense understanding.

I explore all common leitmotifs of the human existence from love to alienation, from bliss in life to decadence and desperation. The action is set up against the luminescent, harmonious, and peaceful background of nature—as a comparison and in contrast. Each trite event from day-to-day living gives me a reason to muse and be amused. And each time I stop to admire a random flower and wonder at a random ray of sun gleaming through clouds, my heart gets filled with hope and light. There is so much beauty in the world to see, to witness, to discover, and to share! And I share it through art, through my verses.

As I live a simple life, I have tried my best to use simple words and simple facts—as common as all the trees and all the grass that we pass by without noticing and appreciating their presence. They look as if lacking any form of poetry. Yet I have found that shade and hue, that beat and sound, that shape and contour, that togetherness and intimacy make each of them stand apart. Each tree and every blade of grass has importance to me. Each hides within a distinct and remarkable universe. Each adds perspective and dimension to human life. Sometimes, however, a longing for my mother tongue pulls me toward words of Latin origin which, it is my hope, brings a soft musicality to my verse and opens new patches of symbolism and meaning.

While many times I capture the familiar and the general in all of us, sometimes I plainly paint self-portraits, exposing all my guts. I believe that many people will relate to what they resonate with in my poems, to what they feel is alike, but sometimes, a new window will open that will reveal to them an unlikely, perhaps unexpected horizon. I talk about cultures and civilizations, generalizations of generalizations, and sometimes I go back to my roots in life and revisit particularities of particularities. I acclaim the picturesque land of my birth, surrounded by majestic mountains, a heaven on Earth, and at the same time I cry out, pointing to the prison I grew up in—an era of utter darkness under a repressive communist regime. Both gave me eyes to see, on one hand, beauty in nature and in all of us; on the other, the condition of the human social-order with its oppressors and its oppressed.

I choose to write my poems in three lines—and only three—arranged in series of sixty, not more and not less. But within this rigid arrangement that gave me peace of mind and structure within a set structure, my playfulness as a form of expression flows freely. Some poems start with the same phrase or end with the same line; other poems congregate on the same theme; some will be exactly in eidetic contrast to each other, and many will stand on their own. And I had so much joy exploring each form. I enjoyed playing with words as well; some selections were purely accidental, although not without value and charm, while others were just the opposite, handpicked after hours of attentive consideration.

My utterances do not represent a final word, but rather a realm caught in the process of transformation as I evolve and as the world itself evolves. Each one seizes a thought or a feeling or both. Together, they convey a life story of being and growing as an artist, as a person, as a soul. They cover a short timeframe, from October of 2014 until June 2016, following the seasons twice through sunny and rainy days. It all started with a request from a friend: "Please send me some poems," she said. "They are inspiring."

"Okay," I replied, "I will."

I guess she chose the right words to get me going, as it seems that I value highly seeking and desiring to simply be inspiring. It is not that I wouldn't have written anyway, but that I was inconsistent in my writing. I will start and abysmal shadows will block my way through. But all of a sudden, something changed in my heart; a veil was lifted and I saw the rays of light falling upon me for the first time. My whole being was vibrating to the call that I had since before birth—to write—and this time I chose to confront my demons instead of running away and hiding. I pushed them off and off and off till over the finish line, till over the mountains, till over the edge of the earth, I threw them out of my universe and my imagination soared freely, unrestrained and unafraid.

Personally, I recommend my verses to poetry lovers, yet I recommend them to poetry nonlovers even more so. My discourse is disentangled from schooled and scholarly rules and regulations, presenting an idea in a raw yet pristine form. I write not as a stylish connoisseur, but as a valiant, wandering troubadour. I write from the heart to touch hearts. It is my hope that my verses will stand as a testimonial, as a cornerstone in bringing about new renaissance in poetry.

Please use the free space on each page to draw or jot down your own reflections, as the readings might inspire you!

Ready to Fly

Ready to Fly

Autumn has come, it seems much too early.
With open wings, my son is about to soar high in the sky.
In this transcendent moment, wordless, both of us rely on faith!

Winking Stars

Teenagers at night sit in the garden about a bonfire.
Raw, fresh dreams hiss in the bluish flames of lumber.
The stars wink above their heads.

Cold Days Melancholy

The temperature dropped all of a sudden.
All the greenery is frozen in a spell, and for a minute
I wish the time would stand still as well.

Transient

Appreciating the snowfall's peacefulness
doesn't make the cold less brutal. Such is the irony of life,
transmuting our soul through a transient love-hate incertitude!

Ordinary

We all remark irises, thanks to Van Gogh.
His touch conveyed so well the extraordinary of the ordinary.
What if we each could find that magic voice within us?

Seedtime

All trees in the winter hold their buds, set to bloom
as soon as the spring heat descends from the Heavens.
The same, I hope the freeze from my heart will melt…

Carpathian *Immortelle de Neige*

Up on the peak of the mountains where no path can lead you,
where the Earth and the Heavens become one in the mist, stands alone,
in rarefied air, a rugged though delicate *immortelle de neige*.

The Obvious

We are looking so hard to find what is right in front of our eyes.
In spite of the obvious, we think that it must be something beyond the blue skies.
We always forget to BE in our heart—Love is all there is and is meant to be—LOVE!

Freefall

I finally learned that there is nothing I can lose by surrendering.
I am letting myself freefall like a feather, without any resistance or regret,
with my eyes open and a big smile on my face, engulfed in heavenly peacefulness!

Under the Rays of Sun

The light of the summer is getting dimmer and dimmer.
I am at a place in life where I find nothing to run from or for anymore.
Just *being* suffices, in the soothing rays of sun.

Tunes of Wind

My pupil asked me, "Teacher, what music are you listening to?"
"None," I said. "The tunes I pay attention to are out of this material world.
All that I hear is the wind whispering songs of harmony, compassion, and love!"

Another Way

Far too often, my students mutter, "Why do we have to do this or learn that?"
Far too often, I would like to tell them, "Please, show me a different way to grow and survive. I yearn to discover that better, easier, more gratifying path myself!"

Dare to Live Powerfully

Last night the skies thundered briskly with a blast so intense
it could have awakened the living out of their lifeless ways!
"I summon Thee," it said. "I summon Thee to Live as Powerfully!"

Restlessness

The path that you did not dare to take will continue to lurk
in the shadow of your mind, alluring you, always hungry to manifest.
That uneasiness will follow you, like a stray wolf, to your deathbed!

Waves

At times, the universe bleeds through me words of wisdom. When I am letting my soul open to the waves, unbound thoughts, feelings, and intentions flow freely. No glory is of Man. At his best, Man can only grasp and honor what Exists since before time!

Drip-Drop

Drip-drop, our minutes on Earth are numbered, drip-drop…
What to Do, what to Be? Drip-drop. Time passes. Drip-drop. One step more, one more breath, one more chance to find faith… Time passes too fast, anyway!

Iris Immortality

Like an iris that blooms a second time a year,
I would like to have a second chance to love. And possible it is,
in the right warmth, in the right ground, with the right care…

Reverberation

Art has a life of its own, like ripples circling the pebble one throws in still waters. And while the artist's intentions die unknown, the waves a-flowing to new horizons, touching all in their path. Art is a reverberation of the original creation, an *aide-mémoire*.

What Lies Beyond

So little of the splendor we see can be captured in a notable photograph; even less so can shine in colors on a canvas. The wonder lies in the twist Man gives to what Man sees. The wonder rests in what the art can reveal!

Preordained

The blood of our ancestors revolves with the clouds in an amassed consciousness, dragging behind archetypes and preordained thoughts about the world, life, and love. And sometimes, it rains. And somehow, it quiets the howls!

The Message

The flower does not cease budding just because it doesn't seem to make any difference in the world. The difference happened with its befalling. And each blossom adds to the beauty of life! Bees and butterflies rejoice!

Beating Hearts

What looks real might actually be not. But what feels deeply—the love and the fear, the fire within us and the light, the search and the fight—is what truly defines us. I see a sky full of hearts beating, connected in an audible chain of pulsations…

Personal Choice

Nobody knows if the ant is happy or not. The ant is carrying out its purpose within its nest. Looking down upon them, the happiness of any individual seems irrelevant. We could infer that happiness is a discernment from within. It is not granted, but rather handpicked.

Nothing to Hide

I can never get tired of watching the rays of sun plunging through clouds. In the light of the day, ever mesmerized, I am walking naked in the Garden of Eden. It is not that I am perfect, but rather because of how imperfect I am that I have nothing to hide.

Binds

Man cannot do good deeds on his own. It is because of the multitude of contexts that evade his sight. It is because the attachment to his ego hinders his tries. It is from standing alone in the fight; alone, insecure, and frightened…

Listen

Pours! Taps on tops of roofs, on the concrete of the roads, on the metallic frames of the cars. The nature has its rhythm. Pause sometimes from your busy life and listen, just listen to the beat of life!

For the Love of Another

And if you are afraid of disappointment, then better stay alone…
And if you are afraid of enduring, then better stay alone…
Love for another comes with turmoil. Accept it, overcome it, or be alone.

For What I Am

How much can I teach a child? My words of wisdom have no weight.
What I stand for brings no change. My toils and struggles have no impact.
I work through, still, for what I am might ring one day in someone's heart!

Glorious

What richness, what glorious richness comes from all the cultures
of the world! Yet so poor in spirit Man chooses to be. Without sharing,
Man stands alone in his glee and alone in his sorrows!

Wounds

A word, an image, a feeling can break loose stiches and reopen old wounds.
The pain, two folded, like a mist reenters the chambers of the soul and floods its dwelling.
With a needle, I sew back the stiches. Debris lies everywhere, but I can walk again.

The Poet

There is no pain a poet didn't bear. There is no sorrow a poet doesn't know.
From deepest hurt and drawn-out mourning, his verse is born. Through all the ache,
he sees all grandeur, and finds in blackness stars before they flicker for their very first time.

Despite an Elusory Nature

I spotted in the crowd a toddler dressed up like Cupid with white wings and a red bow.
I searched up close and far away, but he was gone in the mist, as elusory as he came.
Despite, my heart was left behind, throbbing. I burn in flames, full of love and gratitude!

Pirouettes

Leaves drift graciously to their grave. Their final pirouette goes down in full colors!
Each fall, a life-cycle end designates the start of a new one! Each fall, I witness it, yet
I cannot grasp my own drift to my grave. My first dance would also be my last!

Luminescent

The stars look brighter in a cold night's sky. It is something about that crisp air that makes them shine brighter upon us. The light is always more poignant when lancing through the deepest pit of darkness.

The Children of All

The sorrow I felt in my youth for the pain endured by the children of our world is the same sorrow I feel as I am aging for all the suffering that goes on around us. And our world will never change till we learn to care for the children of all!

Dreams in the Womb

So many dreams die unborn! Like a poem half written or a painting in sketch, a dream in itself has no voice. And although one flower conveys hope, it is a field full of blossoms that stirs attention and makes a statement to the world!

Falling Leaves

So what I dared to dream, if I let my musings die in the wind?
So what I dared to paint or to write, if I kept my work in the dark?
Without sharing, all is but a fall, a fading without the promise of springtime!

The Right Angle

The autumn light is the most spectacular of all. Perhaps it is the vivid colors of the trees that heighten it, or the slightly extra-warm orangey hue of the sun and the softness of its heat. I personally believe it is rather the angle the rays fall upon entities that makes all the difference!

In the Body

I scrutinize the surface of the lake where the blue sky, the trees, and the sun are reflected. For a moment, I rebel against being enclosed in a membrane and separated from the infinite expansion of my soul. I touch the water and I remember why I had to live in a form!

Remember to Live

Skip and whistle on a sunny day. Hip-hop. Chirp-chirp. Crush—crunch. Step over dry leaves. This is what it means to be alive and by all means, it is not little at all!

Harvest

Every year comes a time of harvest when Man unclothes himself, weighs in a year's yielding, readjusts, tunes one's own settings, reassesses the meaning of one's own life… and leaves are dancing in the sky.

Growing Medium

Ideas cannot spring in nothingness. Crude, organic matter is dropped in first; the more meaningful the information added to the pot, the richer the compost becomes, more absorbent as a growing medium. Then and only then can ideas sprout into the light!

Quintessence

A *Ginkgo biloba* and an oak tree stand one by one, more alike than different. Our humanity, just the same, is far more noteworthy than our individual outlooks and physical appearances!

Unassigned

The poems I write resemble colorful paintings. They don't rely on a convoluted play of words, but rather on raw feelings and images. Behold, a smile is hanging on an empty wall, on a paper, on a cloud... without any hidden meaning or purpose.

Free from Answers

Open-ended questions are like eyes in the sky in which one can get lost for eons, ruminating aimlessly. Sometimes it is good to close the question like a door, as sometimes answers don't matter. Sometimes it is good to presume nothing.

Crumbling Questions

From youth, questions keep crumbling down like falling stars. "Why and who?" are strong in early spring. Then, "What, where, and when?" will bloom. "How?" will follow and wither away. In the end will come to pass, "To and for whom…?"

Last Question

I wish I had more questions left in my pocket. But I don't. I spent the last one on the apple of knowledge of the good and the bad, of life and of death, of love and of hate. What I have left now is the free choice.

Last One Standing

The cherry tree blooms first in the spring, but also is the first one to lose its leaves. All the others come into flower one by one and pass just the same. The oak tree is last. Holding still, into late autumn, drops its leaves nobly when everything else is long gone.

The Same Moon Shines Above

The ideals of my youth have dropped to the ground like leaves in the fall.
All the grandeur of being and becoming and saving the world has been eroded
by rain, by wind, by disillusions, by drawbacks... Despite, the same moon shines above!

Years Apart

We met again after years and years apart, me and my childhood friend. Our smiles
are not as bright as we remember them. In our eyes still flickers the passion we had
in our youth, pale, diminished by years of trials. Despite, the same moon shines above!

Refined

The ideals of my youth appear to have dropped to the ground like leaves in the fall.
The trials of life polished my sharp edges. The trials of life quieted my restless heart.
Refined, redefined, the ideals live in me, metamorphosed! The moon reflects the same light...

Fairy Tales

The first frost fell today. In the morning's rays, everything was standing still, like in a fairy tale. I took my sword out of the closet, and all in armor, I left to fight life's mythical creatures. Many times, I came home crushed, but sometimes, I won!

Inner Fight

Life seems to be as illusory as a fairy tale. Yet fairy tales are not illusory. Real demons of our mind and our world hold us in chains. With real courage, we can break free and fight life's mythical creatures. Many times, we will crumble in pain, but sometimes, we will win!

Gray Day

Sometimes, the sky is gray. The atmospheric pressure somehow weighs heavy on our shoulders. It thrusts us to retreat in the darkest, coldest corner of our shell, drenched in regrets for all that has passed. Melancholy drizzles over us the whole day.

Gray Skies

Sometimes, the sky is gray. The clouds are filled with water, but their grayness has no connotation attached to it, per se. Yet to us, grayness is an expectation of color turning either way. There is hope for a blue sky, and many times, we hold onto that hope.

Fall Drizzle

Oh, gray skies, let it rain over all that is gone—first steps and first-time discoveries, first love and first victory, first in a series of firsts still waving in the wind.
Let it cry till there are no tears left in the clouds. Let it cry till all leaves have fallen.

In the Wind

The leaves have no voice on their own. What animates them is the wind.
In the wind, they rustle, and flutter, and swirl, and fall, and are lifted.
A wave, a flow, a gust is what stirs our heart and prompts us to resonate!

A Nest

A nest remained in a tree, visible only now as all the leaves dropped free.
A bird that sang on its branches, put each twig just right for it to hold precious life.
A possibility exists as long as one can envision it; a possibility like an egg in a nest, in a tree …

Interplay

As the rays of sun tilt lower and lower in autumn, the shadows of entities grow longer and longer. Slowly, the umbrae reach further and further. Elusive silhouettes entangle on fallen leaves in an interplay of light and dimness. Reality is what one wants to see.

Hidden Intentions

Suddenly, the quietness of the garden was interrupted. Knock-knock, and then again a double knock, a woodpecker was drumming. Behind was left a hole as big as the bird. Sometimes, hurt is meant to heal. A cutout wound may very well salvage a whole limb.

A Nest

Shattered

Leaves whirl on the ground in the haul of the wind. Vagabonds of late autumn, they rustle as they spin without any particular direction. Our unfulfilled aims drift the same, shattered pages of a book. Ultimately, chilly rain pins them down into a corner.

The Colors of Fall

We were all beautiful at a time of ignorance, and bloomed without knowing. In autumn, we are fading away, while we cannot help but witness it. Yet fall doesn't come without charm. Shorter, colder days are overthrown by a full range of colors.

Time and Again

I opened the door. Rusted leaves rushed in on a gasp of wind. Like emotions of old times, they will linger for a while before they will turn into dust. Definitely, they did their part. I acknowledge their presence time and again, in reverence.

Confronting Adversity

Fall after fall, I look forward to witnessing the moment in which birds are rounding up in the sky and positioning themselves in the optimal assembly to fly. The V formation with its precision of direction fascinates me. But what I admire most is their togetherness in the face of adversity.

Rich Cover

Regardless of size or shape or color, of roughness or finesse, all leaves join together to form a brown, warm, protective cover. They crumble, and grind, and mingle, and fuse into one. Their richness does not end with their fall. Life's abundance continues indefinitely.

A Pattern

Buds flourish in spring, and in autumn, leaves turn colorful and fall … All abide a pattern, in a procession, as if it is meant to tell us something of importance. But life and love and death remain to us as elusive as ever. The wind carries empty thoughts away …

Same Old

I can say nothing new. What is in front of my eyes, I observe, same old, same old… Their undulations reverberate within my depths. I feel and think and react as a human, same old, really, same old. Anew, I sing an ancient song. I am Eve. My offering is an apple.

One Leaf after Another

In how many colors can autumn be painted? In how many tones, hues, palettes? Perhaps it is just a matter of daring endlessness by putting together edge after edge and frontline after frontline. Stroke after stroke, each finite colors the infinite.

Breathing

A leaf doesn't stand for what one can see, but rather concealed attributes make the leaf unique. A leaf's true worth lies beneath. Drop leaves, plummet over Man's soul! As Man breathes in, Man may grasp his own true value, from within.

A Leaf's Message

Tap-tap. Tap. A lost leaf, rusted and crooked and stiff, was beating on the window of my car as I was steering the wheel. Tap-tap. The hour was pounding as well. Tick-tock. "Don't rush through your days," the leaf said, "don't rush. Live fully aware of life!"

Unlock

Open your soul to a new tune or old, a firsthand story, an unfamiliar word, a different language, or just a rustling leaf. As you listen, facets of Being will be revealed to you. Through dark clouds, rays of sun burst without warning. In full light, life shines harmoniously.

Biased Winds

I am no more a tender, shapeless shoot that kneels and bends in the direction of the winds. With branches reaching to the sky and beneath, with deep and strong, established roots, I am a fully grown, upright oak. Now, I laugh at wicked winds.

The Feminine

Nothing embodies the feminine better than the Ocean. It has endless diversity of life, yet fatal perils. Unreachable its depths are, yet peaceful. Restless on the surface, yet the sound of its waves quiets lost souls. Reaches toward travelers' feet, yet never leaves its floor.

Rip Current

Each year, I come to the Ocean to empty my soul of pain and qualms and frustration. The rip current drags my soreness afar. I watch it for a while as it battles to stay afloat. I cut the threads. I let it go. The breeze fills my lungs with a fresh scent of relief.

Transcendental Experience

Any apex comes all of a sudden. Its intensity and uniqueness cannot be predicted, like a sunset at the ocean. The clouds catch on fire unexpectedly. The water and the sky reflect incendiary hues. In that very moment, one is either open to experience glory, or is not.

Broken Shells

Sometimes, beauty shines through broken shells, oddly colored or discolored, indented, marked… The shattered layers expose the inner, flawless build. The same, life passes through Man, engraves all hardships in his heart, and delivers him transformed.

A Life's Longing

The waves spill out endless little treasures. The price is simply paid in wonders. Every man is a little child in his soul, always on the look for that one cherished gem no money can purchase. The waves break. In the light, the foam appears white, white like the purity of Man's search!

Caught Dreams

By the end of fall, a leaf here and there hangs onto branches as if there is still life in them, still something to give. Shadows of their former selves, they are but sorrows of past reveries. Fallen dreams get caught onto branches, as if there is still life in them, still something to give…

A Simple Answer

Why does the leaf have to bud in the spring and grow? 'Cause the tree wants to Be! The same, Man's ultimate purpose is to Exist. Aloneness is his biggest pain; togetherness, his highest aim. Man's search in life is for endless Love. The sand falls merciless in the hourglass, grain by grain.

The Miracle of Life

We were hanging by the fire, me, Mother Nature, and God. "I made all in Heavens and Earth," Father voiced. "I sustain the life you created," Mother whispered in turn. Warming my hands by the flames, I remained quiet. I bring no contribution at all; my existence is a pure miracle!

Unpunctuality

I welcome your tardiness. Patiently, I get to glance for long hours as the daylight gets softer, and to deeply enjoy the colors of autumn with all its shades. I cannot get tired of watching the leaves dance, and spin, and fall, as if life is endless. Thank you, winter, for making me wait!

Blossomless

Does the tree feel any pain as the leaves drop from its stems and the new buds push in? Do fading dreams hurt a man? It is not the falling that burns, but rather the emptiness, the lifeless hollows that remain afterward, as no flower heads will ever replace them!

Overlooked

I remember the springtime's renewed warmth and the petals of cherry blossoms soaring softly. But the long, endless gray and drizzling days, I don't recall as well. The same, the blue skies come to mind from my past, the blue skies and my youthful *joie de vivre!*

Hidden

Winter echoes somehow in man's heart in nostalgic tones. Perhaps are the leafless branches that trigger such perceptions, the desolated landscape, the silenced birds. Unseen, undercover, in a womb, life is actually the liveliest, regrouping, regenerating…

Uniqueness

In spite of apparent closeness, all trees stand alone in a forest. Each will grow on its own and fight for light and water. Although still solitary, Man can hold hands and assist in one another's journey, yet Man walks alone his path, disregarding his unique ability of sharing!

A Day's Sunset

I am writing this poem in the lovely soon-to-be memory of the present. I pursue my wish not as if I will die tomorrow, or in one week, or on the contrary, as if I will live forever, but because this day will pass away by sunset. Now is the time to cherish what one is and has!

Winter Blues

From time to time, painful phantoms of the past will permeate through the membrane of the present. Although it brings forth tangible feelings, it has no link to current reality. A smell, sound, rain, gray, or coldness, maybe, triggers its shackles. All seem indifferent.

When Man Is in Pain

A wounded arbor forms boundaries around a cut to seal it. That part of the trunk dies, and it is left purposeless within the tree. Comparably, when Man is in pain, life makes no sense to him. His body heals, but scars would remain buried, just to resurface when Man is hurting again.

The White Dream

All was white one early morning, misty, frosted, and silenced like in my childhood's dream. "Am I there?" I wondered. The winter chill exposed the error as my vision was soft and warm. "I am there," I mutter. "I am where I want to be. I am in a white dream, peaceful, hospitable…"

All Our Dreams

Each childhood is marked by a few recurring dreams. Plummeting unstoppably is a common one; another one is soaring above Earth. They likely embody our deepest fears and aims. Occasionally, we dive into one that is personal. Mine is a cozy, white world, in a soft, warm fog!

The Word

What is your word, the lens through which you see the world? That word that defines who you are somehow? That word that is uplifting and gives you will to live? The lack of which causes you to crumble and to sink? That word you were shaped by and are an embodiment of?

The Quest for Perfection

Perfection made The Human Being in His image. It shows a feminine side, long suffering, kind, loving; and a masculine one, righteous, strong, determined—an androgynous spirit. The seed of Humankind was split in two. Flawed, men and women yearn to be delivered whole!

Human's Treasure

Genderless, colorless, penniless the human spirit is. Some stand more grounded like stones, others flow like water, bloom like flowers, fly like winged beings… and there is a need and a place for all. Humans, it is time to cherish our souls!

Slumbering Angels

Children are born with a kernel of purpose inside. Many forget what it is they are supposed to find and to do in this life.
Each man is a slumbering angel. Awaken! Deliver your message!

Fruitless Seeds

I see seeds falling from the blue, each one bearing different gifts.
I see them: lovely sprouts in early spring, growing, blooming.
Many wither and fade away, fruitless. The skies are weeping heavily.

Unless

And if human spirits go somewhere after death, they must have come from somewhere prior to their birth. And if all is just a passing from one presence to another face, then a beginning cannot be unless there is also an end.

The Innate Song

The more I listen to the native songs of the world, the more I resonate with each, and the more I distinguish resemblances within us all. In unison, humankind becomes one single voice. Together, we live on the same beautiful planet and withstand the same tryouts.

Traditions

People sing with pride from the deepest realms of their souls—an echo of the times that passed and also of the times to come. Ancestors chant native songs alongside the not-yet born. Ultimately, traditions are created as a means for us to persist and bond.

When Compassion Is Forgotten

When compassion is forgotten, not even one person understands even one person. Disheartening life feels, in pervasive pain, full of uncertainty and loneliness. One single act of kindness from within oneself can banish the harshest desolation.

Toward New Horizons

I read what I understand, but I read what I don't understand even more so.
What I understand connects me with what was, is, I experience, I think.
What I don't understand pushes me over limits, toward new horizons.

Openness

On occasion, as I lie serenely on a bench, answers stumble upon my feet
like leaves in autumn gusted by the wind. Unbiased, they look for a portal in the
feeling-thought space. I pick a leaf, and then another, with eyes full of a child's wonder ...

Search for Meaning

What is my purpose in life? people always wonder. As we gather riches, build castles,
advance in careers, make profitable networks, a meaning continues to elude us.
What if we would stop hustling for more and take our time to give back instead? What if?

For the Sake of Another

From time to time, remember to throw pebbles in the water. The same, remember to put forth a pure effort for the sake of another. The ripples of your act will extend farther and farther to reach and inspire beyond what you can ever imagine.

The Echo of Rain Droplets

It rained straight for five days. The skies were dark and all looked gray.
In times like these, of falling inside interminably, inconsolably, one cannot but ponder, "What would happen if I stop fighting?" There is no answer, only the echo of droplets…

Unknown Calling

The weight of my own thoughts crushes me. At times, I see no sense in all that I do, and I melt down. I look up at the blue sky and I understand that a meaning is not for me to find. Through faith, I am supposed to follow my call, blindly.

The Chosen Dream

Three angels visited me one winter night. The Angel of Peace fondled my hair.
The Angel of Joy led me in a twirl. The Angel of Love kissed my eyelids.
In that mystical light, I fell asleep. If life is a dream, then I choose mine to be this one!

The Mystery of Living

It is a fight to stay afloat more so than to let life go from our hands. Cell by cell,
our body is fading. Why are we alive just to pass away? Why must we die
just to find our life? Perhaps this very mystery makes life worth living and dying for!

The Trap

I sipped a hot chocolate at a café and silently watched. People came in and left;
left and others came in. For a moment, we shared the same space and time,
fully unaware, fully detached. Trapped inside our own thoughts, we forgot to smile.

Castles in the Air

In the winter, time seems to flow differently. The light is dim and darkness falls early upon us. Days and nights merge until we cannot tell anymore if the dawn is pending, or the dusk. We hide inside, behind manmade beams, and dream of castles in the air!

The Memory of Theseus's Ship

Consider the memory of an original ship after all parts have been replaced. Consider the feelings that arise when steering it, the smell, the touch... It compares to the memory of love. Love is the same to us if it resembles the love from our youth—what a subjective twist!

Fireworks

I was expecting the New Year with colored lights and fireworks.
However, in that infinitesimal moment of its passing, I must have blinked!
The footprints of the past are fading... Regardless, we cannot but step forward!

Only Now

Time is only a mark on a calendar. In fact, we start somewhere and we end up, aged, in the same place. If time makes a loop, like in a Möbius strip, the universe is bound to return to its beginning sooner or later. Nonetheless, the present is undeniably irreplaceable.

Collective Corpus

Roots and trunks upright, oblique, or fallen, twigs and branches, dead and alive, all coexist in a forest, amalgamated as one. Nature's richness doesn't come from any single individuality, but from all the plants as a collective mass.

Consciousness Corpus

All fauna and flora, dead and alive, coexist in a forest. Together they represent the richness of life. The same, the value of humanity doesn't come from any single one of us, individually. Our egos are not of relevance, but our devotedness to one collective, conscious mass.

The Sound of Life

In a random winter day, in a random forest, random naked twigs and branches interweave each other in a web under an overcast sky. The bareness of woodlands has a unique, silent ring to it. Listening, motionless like a tree, I heard my own life, breathing!

On a Man's Flyway

As migratory birds have within a finely tuned sense of direction toward their breeding or wintering lands, so man has an internal sense of righteousness. Each year in their flyway, many birds fall prey. On man's path to light, slayers of human souls hunt as well.

Your Best Ally

Listen to your gut. It is by far easier to correct your candid error than to be led amiss by others, on paths you have never thought to follow. In a murky, clouded night, any opinion might sound right. Only your instinct knows your heart, only your holy makeup!

Reverence

Who helps you get up in the morning and sleep restfully at night?
Who is there to hold your hand through hardships and good times?
Who caresses you when crying in anguish? The Venerated One!

Like the Weather

Man is like the weather, rather capricious than truthful, rather too cold or too hot, dry or humid, gloomy or blinding, moving with or against you! The weather breathes its own life with its own agenda, its own winds and rains. The human being endures alone in the torrent.

Of Essence

Understanding nature and human nature is paramount. Nature—to learn to read it, the times, the flow, the land, all life. Human nature—to know what to ask and more so, what not to; what to expect and more so, what not to; what to grant and more so, what not to give away!

Water

The Water and the Mountain

The man is like a mountain, rising majestic, with changing biomes, barren and frozen on its peaks, but with breathtaking views! The woman is like the water in all forms, mysterious, pouring and crashing forcefully at times, also flowing, embracing, soothing…

Intimacy

Perhaps the water is nothing without the ground that gives her shape and the rocks over which she gurgles in her way. Perhaps the mountain is nothing without the water that sculpts his edges and animates his heights. Both, jointly, carry on the life!

Aqua Pura

In pilgrimage, to sacred grounds people journey each year to find wisdom and harmony. Somehow, around water springs, the holy lands are set. The soft murmur, the air about, the solitude maybe in the presence of God, cleanses the body and purifies the soul.

Ingrained

Joy or sorrow is not determined by the gloominess or the brightness of a day,
but rather it sparks inside one's frame of mind. The same, joy or sorrow does not spring
from opportunities or the lack of them, but from one's ingrained take on the matter at hand.

La Femme Divine

My heart mourns the girlish air that I lost—an embodiment, the allure of an angel
full of virtues and of love. A femme divine I will always be, even though
my feminine innocence will pass unnoticed in the shadow of an aging form.

A Woman's Tears

"The divine femme within you is not dying with age," the water relentlessly murmurs.
"Your core is increasingly shining as from a spring; you are becoming an ocean!
Even your tears are not spilled in vain. They add emotions to the barren lands of man!"

Beyond Self-Doubt

Insecure, a woman holds tight to her youthful look. Surpassing her self-doubt, she acknowledges that a youthful look is what people want to see.
Surpassing her self-doubt, she will learn to portray and rely on what she is!

Furs of Snow

It is such a quietness outside. White clouds burst into
little furs of snow. I see them dancing softly in the paleness
of the background. As they touch my hand, they vanish. So is time!

Part of Nature

On a forest trail, I stopped by speechless, naked trees. I grabbed bark
from the woods and with my saliva, I lodged it to my body. I grew roots in time
and become part of nature. Together we live, together we die. Our lives intertwine.

Undisturbed

Any path in the woods is lost in late fall, covered with rusted foliage and broken tree limbs. Behind my steps, I could hear their rustle as they withdrew into an immortal-like state. Back into silence, all sank after my departure. In the continuum of life, I am but a leaf.

Trickle

As long as I expected perfection, I could never finish anything I undertook. As soon as I recognized and accepted limitation and inadequacy, my writing started to flow. It is only a little trickle, flawed but limpid, crude but vivid.

A White Beginning

A blue sky stirs feelings of liveliness and joy, while the gray one brings misery and gloom. But the white, the misty white one, holds no thought. White is the reflection of all colors to the eye and all emotions to the soul. White is the embryonic repose before the beginning.

Before

It must have been white before... The world must have been white and white must have been one and all, pacific, carrying within the seed of potentiality. And darkness was not existent in those beginnings...

Imbalance

Before the molding of man and all life-forms, before the origin of Earth, before the birth of planets and stars, before the primordial burst, angels have fallen. Is it possible that the Universe formed to correct this error? Angels dropped and the world turned uneven!

Human Hearts

Although frail and insignificant by oneself, man as humanity has the potential for greatness. The world itself is shaped by human hearts joined together. The fight of each soul, for each soul is heavy, as each one adds to the white cloud of love and light!

Away from Darkness

How afraid are young children of darkness and thunder! They must have seen none, in the place from where they came. As they grow and become familiar with the world, with all its pains and perils, they dread darkness no more, yet from there on, they should truly fear it!

Twists and Quirks

The migratory birds forgot to fly south this year, and the tree buds, heavily pregnant, are about to bloom in the middle of the winter. Nature seems to be at odds with its habitual rhythm. It reminds us that nothing is set in stone. Twists and quirks are part of life as well.

Ephemeral Shell

When young and inexperienced, we feel invincible. Later on, physical pains remind us how fragile we are, and short lived, like a flower. We see it blooming, enjoy its beauty, and the very next day, we witness it wither in front of our eyes!

Glowing Shell

When young and inexperienced, we feel invincible. Later on, physical pains remind us how fragile we are and short lived, like a flower. If we would learn early on to ever-so-gently caress our being, we will wilt even so, but with a smile on our face!

Portrayal

From the smooth surface of the young sprout, in time, the bark becomes all wrinkled and crumbled. Each crease, however, is a day in which the tree fought to be and become, is a day the tree succeeded in being and becoming!

Reverberation

I listen to the same tunes for days and days, till they become part of myself. All of a sudden, my inner vibration changes, and I resonate with something else for days and days, till it becomes part of myself!

The Endless Beyond

I never know exactly what I am looking for, but I know that I am seeking into "the beyond" with high intensity and restlessness till I fall over the edges of my own limited perceptions. For one day, I am happy with my findings; then I am on the move again!

Disjointed

We live in ignorance these days, so detached, so disconnected from our inner selves and our surroundings. As a branch cut from the tree of life, we are already dead while still breathing. Separated, in isolation from nature, we cannot exist!

Brazenness

Without concerns, we let everything die around us. Clean water, the plants, the wild animals are vanishing fast. The sky is about to break in two for our shamelessly callous lifeways. Despite an obvious fate spun from our doings, or lack of them, we choose to go by, detached…

From the Top of a Mountain

From the top of a mountain, everything looks uplifting and peaceful.
From the top of a mountain, the view is an omnipresent, clear-cut splendor apart from the obscure entanglement of its foothills. Inside us soars a mountain as well.

True Self

Search through every corner of your depths and climb every ridge of your heights.
Poke around, remove each veil, wander and get lost with the curiosity of a child.
You will find in the bottomless you, not only yourself, but also an entire majestic universe!

Torn Apart

I am torn apart between the longing for companionship and the need
to dwell alone, within myself. I want touch and hugs and kisses and
on the other hand, by myself, I am at peace. Lost, I can get on either path.

In Full Light

The shadow is weak in the light. The light is pale in the shadow. Standing upright, exactly under its source, man's shadow vanishes fully. The further man removes himself from that brightness, the shadow grows longer, darker, creepier, overpowering…

Warm Touch

All that I wanted in my youth was to give and give and give till nothing was left of myself, the same as a cloud would pelt down all its holding droplets. The blue sky started slowly to be revealed as I rained and I rained for days and years. A ray of sun fell upon me, tenderly!

Without Expectations

What held me back doesn't have power over me anymore. I finally found the freedom I always had, within myself. I soar, like in my childhood dreams, without fears and without expectations. I fly on a warm current with my eyes open!

Sharing Oneself

You don't have to be affluent to live in abundance! Wealth comes from all the ideas and emotions one gathers and expresses. Riches stem from what one does, from how much one smiles and loves, and from how much one shares of oneself...

Sprouting

I unveiled too little of myself, an end that I fully regret. If this is a last moment before the last moment, I rise from my knees and share my heart, holding nothing back! It is not raining in vain. Buds will be sprouting soon...

Hidden Currents

The trees bow as the winds blow. And clouds are puffed in all directions. And storms are upheld, and storms are appeased; all pushed by drifts invisible to the naked eye. In the spirit world, currents press on just the same.

Into the Storm of Life

Like a boat without a captain, people drift away aimlessly into the ocean. "Awaken," the storm utters amidst the uproars of waves and thunders. "Assume responsibility, and rise up to your given freedom to choose your way and your endpoint!"

Far Reaching

The more challenging the search to find your way at sea, the more enriching your journeying will be. With the wind in your chest, the stronger you will become, the more determined and skillful to navigate further, to lands no one reached before!

A Woman's Muse

From past and past and longtime past, men have been charmed by beautiful, divine beings, and inspired to great creations. Bemused, I muse as to whom might be my own muse? Amused I am by the thought that a woman's muse is her own self!

Hope

We are able to endure the coldness and desolation of the winter because of the hope of springtime, with the warmth, colorful blossoms, and all the buzz that comes with renewed life and love. Without that hope, existence crashes bones!

Unlikelihood

Words describe well the physical reality, but the inner one, less so. Science plays with quantifiable measures of the world, but the inner universe remains less known. Truthfully, man should never be able to calculate and foretell another man's soul!

True Identity

I am a soul. I live as a soul. I feed and groom my soul. Acknowledging other souls, human and nonhuman, I exchange positive vibrations with all. I love living as a soul. I experience feelings of uplifting wellness and joy. This is my true identity. I am a soul.

The Fight for Free Will

I am in the middle of a storm at times. Lightning strikes from every direction, and the wind knocks me down. "Appease," I say, "appease!" The electrochemical processes in the brain subdue. In spite of pushes and pulls from many forces at play, the human can choose!

Morning Mourn

I am on the brink of giving up to this free will of getting up early, while the night is still up. My morning just died around the smell of bitter coffee. And now that the requiem is through, I can choose to either mourn or find some delight in the rest of the day.

Tentative Prognosis

The blooms in spring forecast the harvest to be in the fall. Yet many flowers die without yields. Some are not meant to be. But for the most part, the bees and the effort one carries during the long days of summer tally for the difference!

One in One Hundred

Countless buds sprout on branches, but many won't bloom. From the ones that get to flower, many will drop barren, soon. From the remaining fertile ones, many will fade away. From those that are growing still, to worms and fowls they might fall prey. Only one in a hundred will ripen.

Priorities

Worries! Worries... Inexplicably, we worry about the lack of time to attend to what we hold dear. Inexplicably, giving priority exactly to what makes us, US, is the unshakable way to reaching any accomplishment in a day's toil.

Free-Flow Elegance

The free-flowing, untouched, natural bed of a waterway enchants our eye the most. Any raw intricacy of the stream adds to its charm. The same, when I don't think at all about what I write, my verse emerges at its best.

Obtuseness

Each facet of the diamond shines brightly up in the sky. It captivates and blinds us equally. Seduced by the glimpse we catch from our narrow angle, with impudence we think we have grasped its essence. The uncut truth is in all facets of the diamond put together.

Soft Spot

I saw it; each man has a soft spot in his heart. Afraid of being hurt,
and withdrawn into a dark corner, like a snail in a shell, each human,
no matter how strong in appearance, yearns to be discovered and loved.

Emptiness

I decided to believe in love. I can lose nothing, but rather
find my heart on the edge of the river of time.
Empty it flows without love, empty…

Two

Love is like imaginary numbers—two are needed to become real. By itself, love is a purely abstract, impersonal concept, drifting among stars.

Drizzling Days

I hide well the loneliness feeling that chases me. No matter how fast I run, in endless, drizzling days of early spring, loneliness catches up with me, eventually. Helpless, I fall into its arms. Inconsolably, I cry drizzling, endless days of early spring.

Insomnia

I didn't sleep at all last night. A trouble deep inside kept me up. I turned and tossed and talked it through, but the struggle within did not back up, did not withdraw. In flames, it consumed my buried feelings and thoughts. By morning, only ashes were left in the pit.

Full Moon

Tonight is a full moon. I know it from the restlessness of my heart. My blood, in tune with the ocean, responds to its call. All dormant longings and yearnings and aches of my body awaken. It is then that I feel the most my bond to Earth, and the Sun, and the Moon...

The Meaning of Words

Words have no meaning. They are just empty shells. On the other hand, we assign meanings to words. Some meanings are much bigger than any word can contain. When we express those words, their essence overflows into infinity. Such is Love.

Before Words

It is true; words have come to us last, after objects, after facts, after feelings, after thoughts, after dreams... after our desire and need to be together and share with another each object, each fact, each feeling, each thought, and each dream!

Creative Flow

Art prevails as a work of habit. The more one expresses oneself, the bigger becomes the main stem gushing from the creative spring. Tributaries, as new sources of inspiration, will add to the flow. And nothing can stop the current!

"About to"

I love the "about to" moments; about to crack for dawn, the wave about to break, buds about to bloom... The "about to" apnea is a standstill in the continuum of time. I cherish the wait, the "about to" singularity that is "about to" reach for my heart!

A Miraculous Life

Every "about to" is a marvel of life; about to fall in love, about to see an idea through, about to snow... Each "about to" represents an abrupt change from a form to another. Existence is a series of miraculous transmutations.

Moment of Hibernation

Just like that, the landscape changed from white clouds pressuring from above, to about-to-snow hesitation, to it is snowing hard. The sound, though, remained the same, quietness from end to end. My dreams will take rest under the cover of white for now!

Snows in Silence

I found no other perfect sound or the perfect lack of it, as it resonates during a snowburst. The clouds, the flakes, and the newly fallen fluff of snow reflect the vibration of all colors, but absorb the waves of all sounds. The white, surrendering silence is one of life's imponderables!

Singularity

Either full of life or unanimated, every presence is a marvel of work, from its detailed structure to its precise functionality. Our own existence, in spite of felt struggles and hurt, is the most unique miracle of all!

Nihil

Openness

White page, nothingness, lack of feelings, lack of thought, emptiness, or perhaps fullness... Nothing is wiped down though, because nothing existed in the first place. Nothing transpires yet.

Declaration of Purpose

"State your purpose," Nihil requests, "and you shall pass beyond the door of meaninglessness." One has to declare one's purpose in order for it to materialize. Without a *raison d'être*, man walks through life with hollowness in his heart.

The Feeling Comes First

The thought is the aftermath of a feeling. The sentiment comes first, like the lightning before thunder, prompting us to look for a cause. We feel loneliness, and pain, and love, before we are able to ponder!

The Thought Comes First

The thought is leading the dance. How one perceives a situation triggers a feeling that arises afterward. Sentiments are merely reverberations of thought waves bouncing off a barrier. The more distant the concept, the dimmer its echo.

Unpredictable

The more facets a setup has, the less the probability of any outcome.
That is why our life, as humans, has vast possibilities. Our intricacy of thoughts and feelings renders our choices unpredictable. Essentially everything becomes viable!

A Breakthrough

Nothing is set in stone. For each pattern, a mutation always occurs in spite of clearly defined physical laws. Each mutation causes a new set of patterns to form as if the cosmos is made to function flawlessly. In any predictable continuum, a breakthrough is possible!

The Grief of Our Bloodline

We carry in ourselves the pain of our ancestors. Their persecution and torment, their hurt and grief, lives on, hidden in our veins. And sometimes, we find ourselves reacting to some injustice against our own from eons ago. I bow; my blood is tainted as well.

Gateway

I cut the thread of my link to the past all the way to the first in my bloodline. I free myself from the burden I carry within me, all the suffering of my precursors! In the collective consciousness a new opening occurs, a future we can create from the present we choose!

Playing with Words

First of all, children play. They play with toys, tools and pans, twigs and rocks, and even with words. Like any other sparkling object, to discover new words and meanings has to them the same magical appeal. First of all, language develops as an expression of freedom and joy!

Nautilus Shell

Words and expressions are bridges between perceptions and cognition. Each word opens a new window. Each open window expands the border of our intellectual horizon. In turn, each horizon widens our awareness, adding chambers to our inner Nautilus spiral!

Blues of Winter's End

Toward its end, the pallid, cold winter drags its feet straight through one's soul, trailing deep blues. Chills get into bones. It feels as if spring, with its warm light, will never return.

Spring Coming Aura

The last day of winter passed. Snowbells and crocuses announce it together with the restless bird chirping early mornings! With the buds on the trees about to burst, renewed liveliness and hope enrich the spring aura!

Like a Woman

The sea mesmerizes and the moon shines as women do, the seasons, the flowers,
the butterflies, and the muses are embodiments of women, too. Oddly,
the personification of a woman is revered, and not the genuine woman, in blood and flesh.

The Courage to Cry

Real strength one needs to bear pain, to admit one's faults and limitations,
to heal from rejection and discrimination, to suffer for the hurt of others!
Like rain, tears are meant to soothe and cleanse and replenish …

At Odds

As the beginning of each spring comes near, the realization
of time pulling me closer toward my life's end grows pervasive.
The flowering of trees pins down my blossomless existence.

The Yields of a Seed

Will we sprout into the next existence like a shoot in the spring? If we grow from a seed, the time for budding is now, unsealed to absorb all the warmth and light of life and give back the fruits we are made to yield, each and every one of us!

Triad

When a part of the body, mind, or soul hurts, the entire body, mind, and soul suffers indiscriminately. A human ceases to exist as a human if any part of him is disabled. Together, body, mind, soul, they fight to be. Each part is afraid of losing the others!

The Music Box

The music box inside my heart broke. It doesn't play the song of love anymore. Abandoned, lies in a corner, covered in dust and cobwebs, longing for the warm touch of another one's heart...

The Memory of Spring Love

At times, we return to the memory of springtime and spring love. We remember holding hands, kissing for the first time, touching each other tenderly... We all lost love and loved ones, but love has never forsaken us!

All Pervasive

And composers write music inspired from verses; and poetry cadences follow instrumental tempo; and paintings transpose words and sounds in colors. Art, in all forms, portrays the same piercing human sentiments!

Encrypted Message

I am healing from something that happened to me before I can remember, even before I was born. Perhaps it is just the challenge, the primordial trial, with which I had come. I cannot decode its message. Restless, I fight on.

The Fear of Success

The fear of success paralyzes humans' ability to create freely. It raises one's awareness of value and therefore the lack of it. In reality, worth is not significant for art, per se, but rather the courage to express the undefined. Art is a flow from infinity to infinity through one's heart!

The Fear for Failure

The fear of failure impedes the human to live up to what, ultimately, one believes in and sees in one's mind. But in art, exactly the failure from the norm brings uniqueness and daring to any expression. Art is at its finest, in a pristine-imperfectitude form!

Embracing Thy Self

I had come full circle. What mattered to me from the beginning still matters! Regardless of how much I had run or how much I have searched, all roads and trials brought me back to the starting point. I was born what I am. This time around, I will embrace my call!

Promise

I promise to express what emanates from and through my heart without fear, without hesitation, without holding back. I accept to be a messenger of pristine and divine beauty in all forms. I undertake my path with pure faith.

A Little Bit of Warmth

The trees bloomed overnight, and the colorless became colorful! The light brought just enough warmth for buds to venture bursting open. This is exactly what love does to one's soul.

A Halting Point

From time to time, our world gets to a halt. We hit a wall invisible to others, but from inside, crushing us. Although fictional walls can be surpassed by opening fictional doors, we find ourselves at a loss in our mind. To prevail, we need a helping hand.

A Spinning Point

From time to time our world spins uncontrollably, drifting off course. We might recognize the spinoff, yet in the turmoil's whirl, we find nothing to grab onto. Disoriented, we find ourselves lost in our mind. To prevail, we need a helping hand.

Walking on a Narrow Line

The boundary between sane and insane is indistinct. The wild that makes us, us, joyful, unique, and invaluable, is the part that drags us over the limit of sane into our insanity. I walk myself on a narrow line; above is the blue sky, below is the abyss.

Nonexistent Existence

There is a place beyond desperation where no tear is left to be shed. In a darkness so absolute, even the mind turns a black page. It is a nonexistent existence, completely hopeless; a life that is not a life. Wanderer, be wary of the path you take!

Existing Existence

There is a place beyond calmness, full with streams of light. In a grace so absolute, the mind ascends unblemished white. It is an existing existence, completely hopeful; a life full of life. Wanderer, in belief, choose your path!

Into Physical Existence 1

Everything becomes feasible in a dream or in spirit as we lack corporeality. But in a body, in our limited physical body, is where the impossible becomes possible. We touch and we are touched! Perhaps we materialize for this very purpose.

Into Physical Existence 2

Perhaps we materialize for this very purpose, to touch and be touched. Everything that is not feasible in a dream or in spirit becomes possible in a body. Our limited physical body brings to us the impossible!

Into Physical Existence 3

Our spirit struggles, bound to Earth, as urges and desires of the body torment us. Yet for the chance of corporeal touch, we endure all pains. We live and die for the same purpose, to ultimately find pure Love!

Into Physical Existence 4

I am in a body. I am in a body for such a limited time. Is this occurrence something special, I wonder? Something that can only be here and now? I look at my hands and I see value in them. So much more than beautiful flowers we are!

Into Physical Existence 5

Our spirit is passing through a body. We embark on a voyage as an embryo and descend from a crumpled and weary physical form at the end of our journey. All we can do amidst is to breathe in all the sensations that come our way!

Cherry-Blossom White

There is white and then there is cherry-blossom white, with a little touch of pink. Among all blossoms, this stands out the most. Is it the particular shade; is it the flower arrangement on branches; or is it the feeling that it draws in us? Joy and youthful fondness!

That Day

That day, the cherry blossoms were at their peak; fully open but not faded yet. I captured the moment in a frame and hang it in my soul. In that day I walk once in a while, when I need to remember why I should smile and keep going on!

Diaphanous

I touched the cherry blossoms, and the flowers touched my skin, so softly. Diaphanous were its petals, like nothing else, or perhaps as diaphanous as life is. So softly, the flowers touched my skin. Serene, I received their blessing.

A Helping Hand

Yesterday I sponsored a child. Today I planted a tree. Tomorrow
I will save a baby elephant. This is what makes us Human, the ability to act
with intention, with heart, for a harmonious future we envision for all life alike!

The Protector of Life

Any creature is flawlessly made and none is worthless
of their own existence. Above all, Man stands powerful and mighty.
Above all, humanity has the capacity to destroy all life, or protect it!

Together We Live or We Die

To nature we all belong in life and in death. Earth's ecosystem
is conceived as such that humans cannot survive without wildlife.
Caring for our natural world simply means to give ourselves a chance to last.

Passing Trough

At night, the first thunderstorm of the spring fell. The wind ravaged through branches. By morning, the blossom's petals were taken by water. It doesn't matter that they dropped, but rather that they lived and enchanted our sight for a moment!

Birth Land

We are linked to the land we are born into. The setting, with all its particularities, the wildlife, the chirping of birds, the smell of the flowers, is all imprinted in us. And no matter where in this world we venture, our roots will always be there.

The Memory of Our Beginnings

We are linked to the dirt we are born from. All that has significance to us originates in our native land. From there on, we cannot but compare or relate to the memory of beauty as it appeared to us in our beginnings.

Rarefied Air

I am from the mountains and of the mountains. My spiritual existence resides in the rarefied air lost between summits and clouds, surrounded by small, delicate flowers and nomadic sheep flocks.

Fluid Transit

I grew up with the fragrance of white acacia flowers alluring me in spring with dreamy, mystical clouds. Or perhaps it was just the enticement of youth. In another place now, the transience of life, embodied in the passage of cherry blossoms, becomes cloudless!

Perfect Shape

The leaves are emerging in fresh-green tints and maroon hues. They sprout contorted like a closed hand. In a spiral, they open day by day to what shape it is they are meant to take, just perfect and free to absorb all given light.

Immersed in Life

I took a day off routines just to cry, to cry out low and cry out loud. All sorrows and fears came pouring out like a spring rainstorm. In a minute, I was all soaked to the core. It is not a bad thing, I guess. It shows that I am still alive and fully immersed in life!

Contemplation

One should squeeze among daily agendas time to daydream. As unrealistic as it might seem, it is the hour in which awareness of our own unique existence occurs. And perhaps for that very reason, all the stars shine and all the flowers bloom!

A Nail on a Wall

Striking, a nail on a white wall hangs out on its own! It is the witness and the proof of a materialized intention. As I look at it, I envision many uses, yet I like it just the way it is, because it talks to me about possibilities!

Through One's Weakness

Darkness always finds one's feebleness to sneak in and torment one's soul. For some it is the weakness of the body, for others of the heart, for others still, the mind is the one caving in. Darkness is always lurking close by.

Through One's Strength

Light is always invited in by one's strength. Some have a good grip over their body; others rely on their unwavering heart; for others still, the mind is their pillar. Light heals; light caresses; light uplifts one's soul.

Broken Barriers

First, I gave up on the idea of perfection. Then, I didn't care about being accepted or successful anymore. I ended up in total ignorance of what my work would mean to anyone and anything. Free from self-imposed barriers, I am finally Me!

Inimitable Fingerprint

There is a peculiar hum of the Earth, the same blue as its predominant color seen from space. It sounds as a mixture of winds through waves mostly. Everything in cosmos seems to have a voice. Each one of us chants a personal song, engulfed in an inimitable aura.

The Spark of Light

When a myriad of female and male gametes of corals meet, at a particular time, magically set, a flash of light occurs to entice any observer. It is a cue left for us to witness how life emerges, by union, in unison, in the heat of a spark. Life is a miracle of light!

Delicate Distraction

The first butterfly of the year flew by me the other day.
It fluttered its wings around newly blossomed flowers in a strange,
zig-zagging path and then glided away with the wind.

Incoherent Development

It poured straight for seven days. I remember now why, in spite of its springtime beauty, youth felt unbearable. I don't miss a bit all its storms out of the clear, temperature swings, excessive pollen and allergies, crude form of all features, in an incoherent development…

Young at Heart

It poured straight for seven days. I remember now why, in spite of its springtime moodiness, youth can be edifying. The spill of rain is followed by an overwhelming growth and flourishing. A young heart is always open, always searching with sincerity, discovering, forward thinking…

Suitable Background

One day, three, one week maybe; this is how much a flower lasts in spring and a woman's youthful appeal with it. Yet year-round character is given by one-of-a-kind foliage in contrast to a well-chosen background.

I Bow to All

I Bow to All

Today, I am Japanese. Quietly, I observe, and quietly, I take all in. In simple, curved lines I paint my view; add a little bit of red and a little bit of blue. A single word I write with a soft but firm stroke. I pick one flower and one alone. To all, I bow; to all …

The Joy of Being Oneself

I am feeling rather French at times, quite fond of being frankly odd. I *parlé* this and *parlé* that, showing off my *joie de vivre* in all I do. With thick strokes and vivid colors, I choose to paint the world each time from a different slant. Intensely, I live my given *liberté*…

Incorrigibly Romantic

Part of me is Italian, incorrigibly romantic. I find time to smell each flower, as under a plethora of stars, each little thing has value. *Amore* kicks in and brings each day new Renaissance. Life is *bella*, when one loves, life is *bella*!

Belonging

For a day I want to be Maasai, the warrior, the shepherd, and the protector of wildlife. Possessions, age, time have no use to me. I live close to the dirt from which I am made, which gives me shelter and nourishment. An entire tribe is my tending family!

A Humble Life

Humbleness I learn each day, and the care for each creature no matter how small. In peace, I make my statement known as an enlightened Indian showed us, some time ago. I search for the tranquility of sacred places and for the wisdom gathered in ancient manuscripts.

Camaraderie

I will be Slavic too, just to please my Russian friend. From her, I learned that a political regime does not describe a nation, or a culture, or a person. I can read poise in her eyes, and care, and passion. We can all be comrades if we choose so, regardless of what divides us.

All Live in Me

To Sami joiks I relate at times, to Celtic dances, and Islamic drawings full of intricate patterns. Through the mountains I wander like the Mongols and the Altai. I listen to the Mother Earth as Native Indians do, and I belong to the God of the Jews.

All Live in Us

We are all to the Earth and Earth is to us our cradle in life and our resting bed in death. Our blood is nothing more than a rain made out of our ancestors' evaporated tears and sweat. All live in us, pains and joys, in a sealed kinship, from the dawn of our world.

Spiritual Expansion

Fiddleheads, refined yet of a sturdy build, pop out of dirt in spring.
Grounded on earth, they emerge with an air of unrolling confidence.
I strive to unfold in a similar manner, flaunting a continuous golden ratio!

World's Sonata

Fiddleheads, packed in fractals, pop out of dirt all trundled up like a scroll on a violin. Slowly, they are unfurling their young fronds in an inaudible yet magical sonata. No matter from what point of view we look at the world, it cannot show us but divine magnificence.

The Right Time

Plants sprout and flowers bloom at a certain time, each
after its kind. Being late or starting out sooner will cause a chain
of events that might undermine their bearing fruit or ripening.

Contextual Hardships

I was holding the lines of a kite all prepared, standing by to feel any sign from the wind, a gust or a pull hard enough, long enough to keep it uplifted. Upon me had descended solely the realization that it is not all our fault for failing on our dreams, as I thought!

An Artist's Fate

Madame Lebrun didn't live in vain. She expressed what so many other women did not get the chance to: herself! Talented she was indeed, but more so, the circumstances were in her favor. The wind blew in her wings just right. In her art, she was ready to soar!

Graceful Souls

I met the spirit of Emily Dickinson once. Her embodiment had the same deep, thoughtful eyes and wrote perfectly conveyed verses as well, full of meaning and character. She kept her poems and her life private. Unknown, she will pass by with grace, as many other Emilys did before her.

Left Behind

Perhaps it is out of the fear of being surpassed that the World of Man pushed its other half in darkness. After all, a woman does not necessarily need worldly knowledge to grow wise or acclaims to feel important. She can reach self-actualization simply by being herself.

The Other Half

What did the World of Man gain by pushing its other half in darkness? More noteworthy, what did humankind lose by doing so, how much knowledge, how much insight, how many marvels of imagination and of the heart? How incomplete the world ever was!

Emerging from Darkness

Women are emerging anew, patching and soothing the World of Man, who kept them in darkness. As they bloom in full light, I do hope their souls will remain more on the kind side than on the proud one, more loving and less disheartening, more patient and less judgmental…

Chauvinism Ashes

I am forgiving the World of Man for all chauvinism and oppression on my fellow womankind. Growing up, it stung me too. Today, ashes I pour over my head and free myself from what was. By spilled dreams and blood of women before me, the world has changed. I did as well!

A World of Compassion

No matter our social class or skin color, no matter our gender or age,
we are born and die, love, suffer, enjoy life, and search for greatness in similar ways.
As a world, it is time to foster and praise the compassion in us, and endurance, and devotion!

The Nameless Lady

Choose to be a Lady, not through how you look, dress, talk,
or what and how you perform in the face of the world, but through
your gentle touch and caring deeds when nobody is watching at all!

The Friends

When I doubt myself and fall into darkness, I relearn who I am through
the friends I have. When I don't know where to start and what to carry on,
my friends are revealing to me how much more I am and I can do than I think of myself.

The Healer

When I am anxious and at unrest, I step bare into the forest. I touch the water, I listen to birdsongs and to the rustle of leaves, and I find solace amidst, and peace. Mother Nature heals and embraces us all!

The Shield

And when I am crushed to the ground and see no way out into the light, the Heavenly Father is reaching out with might and yanks me back on my feet. As my armor, and shield, and sword, He walks my path before me!

Beyond What Is Seen

My life starts after my job and family time, after chores at home, after my passions and hobbies, beyond traveling and discovering the world, further than hanging out with friends and doing volunteer work. My life opens up where the material actions stop!

Carried Along

I hear the train screeching and puffing in the distance, more clearly at the time between day and night when life gets quiet, not fully asleep yet, nor fully awake. It carries me back toward my childhood, toward my birth, toward the indistinct stars from where I came...

Never-Ending Cycles of Impermanence

Man's mind ventured to the edges of Earth and beyond galaxies in search for immortality. In comparison to our life, the stars look indeed still and timeless. Yet in the material world, immortality exists only in the continuing of life, ending life, life, ending, in never-ending cycles...

The Lure of Distant Stars

Afraid of death, man hunts in all directions of this universe for immortality. He finds hints in poems about distant stars, shining in the concept of eternal Love and in the belief of life beyond life. All that man uncovered in all directions of this universe is the wind...

Passing Moments

I envisioned living endlessly, a life after another. I was a knight or a damsel at times. I reached fame in countless fields, and I relished in many passionate loves. No matter how long I lived though, life was just one, made of passing moments, passing…

Spring Lenses

Like a focus on a camera, our self-image gets stuck at a certain age, in our youth. All the pictures we take from there on lead our eye through that vibrant appearance. We perceive a prolonged spring for the rest of our life.

Dancing Petals

Like a focus on a camera, our self-perception gets stuck at about fourteen years of age, with our emotionality regressing to five at times of distress. Only the mirror shows us an unfamiliar face. Petals fly in the wind as we live on with the illusion of an eternal spring!

Early Spring Bruises 1

As they emerge into this world in early spring, all sprouts, bare and frail, endure sudden temperature falls and high ups, drenching or drought times, overexposure to the ardent sun or rundown in the shadows. None of them escapes unbruised!

Early Spring Bruises 2

Early bruises on sprouts show up in deep, cut scars on the trunk, in lacerations, or sunscalds. But the true sores of human beings lie under the skin, covered by fabricated, self-assuring attitudes. No one escapes childhood unbruised, no one!

Early Spring Bruises 3

How blind and helpless a baby human being comes into this world, how unfit to defend himself and survive! All crashes him suddenly as daunting surroundings and pains. No matter the amount of warmth one is given, he will inevitably feel at times stranded, alone, and uneasy!

Early Spring Bruises 4

I hid my springtime sores in the abyss of my soul. Like sandstorms, they sneak out of the blue to suffocate me. The burst vanishes as it came. I pick up the damages and bury all even deeper. Somehow, they find means to resurface. Childhood bruises never give up their ghost!

Early Spring Bruises 5

Early spring bruises will never give up their ghost. Yet we can grow upright in spite, and nurture in us a human heart, warm, open, and kind. After all, we are the caretakers of our inner meadows and rivers. We can keep them in full light, pristine, filled with flowers!

The Flower

It is not a flower's fault for her grace and beauty! As soon as inadvertently she captivates man's eye, she becomes vulnerable, an object of enticement. Yet man has a choice to break her, step over her, pull her out by the roots, or protect and admire her glory!

A Flower's Crown

The flower buds on her own. She bears as many florets as she can hold.
Some blossoms are pollinated and bear seeds. Then the flower withers,
self-fulfilled. Her crown, once eye catching, lies down on the ground by her youngling.

From the Rim

I am taking my last breath. I either push the artist in me to live or let it rest in peace.
Either way, it makes as much sense to create a corpus of art as it doesn't. Either way, I have
nothing to prove or disprove. All ideas are but clouds in the sky, coming and going freely...

Unresolved

I am taking my last breath, still holding onto what I feel defines
my artistic mien. Every day is empty without my art, hopeless and aloof.
Yet all I can create are but clouds in the sky, coming and going freely...

Light Prevails

There are different levels of infinity as there are different shades of color. The discrete components make all the difference between love and hate or light and darkness. As the light spectrum is vastly larger than the dark one, the same is its level of infinity.

Celestial Roots

As if we fell from the blue, we emerge into this realm, inverted. Our eyes as well look at the world upside down, for the right side up is meant to be toward the sky. From there on, we lose sight of our celestial roots and revert to earthly bound beings!

Upside Down

I used to walk upside down in my youth, jumping from cloud to cloud. On the wing, the Earth looked incredibly pristine. It wasn't meant to be, I guess, as life pulled me low, into a quotidian vortex. But at night, when nobody is around, I still dance upside down.

After the Rain

Decomposers go by mostly unnoticed, although, in the great scheme of our universe, it is the one entity to show us clearly how nothing is lost, but rather processed and recycled to be used and materialized into something new. In a forest, mushrooms surface after rain.

After a Nonphysical Rain

What if our spirit decomposes the same way as our body, playfully I wonder? Our consciousness would be broken down into essential components and rearranged in a collective-consciousness cloud. In a nonphysical forest, mushrooms surface after rain.

After an Emotional Rain

After an emotional rain, mushrooms surface in the dampness of the forest, decomposing all feelings and thoughts into something unrecognizable. What we will remember might have only little likeness with the original rupture.

An Artist's Testimonial

I am in touch with the Divine through the breathtaking beauty I see. Patterns, colors, light, textures, liveliness, strength, grace, love—this is what I portray and share with the world—a piece of celestial perfection expressed in an imperfect way!

Unfounded Hesitations

Three shadows followed me as an artist: the purpose with the intention of acting on it, the worth with the quality of the expression, and the meaning with its importance in making a difference. They are my deepest doubts and obstacles. Unfounded, they still tail my steps.

The Elements 1

The dirt is for toiling with our hands; a sweat that earns us our survival on Earth. The water is for cleaning ourselves and all that we touch, and for purifying our depths. The fire brings us together and warms us at night. But the wind, the wind is for joy and fun!

The Elements 2

Be stable and firm, a pillar of strength, like the earth. Be versatile like the water, never giving up, always finding a way, bending but not losing essence. Be lively like the fire, passionate in all you do. But like a spirited wind, wander, search, try, discover!

The Elements 3

Listen to the earth, to the breathing of life cuddling at its breast. Listen to the appeasing coos of water and its flowing guidance. Listen to the fire cracking; burn all resentments to allow each day to be a new dawn of hope. To the wind's whisper listen, calling unto you…

The Elements 4

Holy is the dirt from which we were molded. Holy is the water with the blessings poured over us. Through the holy fire of a burning bush we deliver our soul, unbroken. With a breath of air, the Holy Spirit uplifts our being to the skies.

The Elements 5

Do not live in filthiness. Do not stir the waters. Do not provoke the fire.
And do not add to the winds. Everything that sustains life can also destroy it.
Everything beautiful can be tarnished. Take each step without leaving dents behind you.

What If?

What if we smile at each passerby? What if we give a hand to the fallen ones?
What if we show care for our surroundings? What if we give ourselves another chance
to be, to love, to do more, better, with all our heart? I bet our skies would be brighter!

A Child's Soul

Learn from the child within to keep "what if" flames alive. Without "what ifs"
our horizon diminishes to a trite life, closed and dull. We can dream and aspire
to new heights at any age. We can certainly fly. To where is up to each one of us!

Walking Together 1

Be there for the child within when he is scared or cries. His hurt is deep and truthful. Whisper to him tenderly reassuring words like, "I understand your pain and I am here for you!" As you learn to walk together, hand in hand, the child within will bloom.

Walking Together 2

Follow the child within. He will run by springs of clean water and woodland meadows full of light and wildflowers. From a peak of a mountain, he will show you the majesty of the world. As you learn to walk together, hand in hand, your whole being will blossom.

Shedding Our Skin

From a distance, the teenage years remain a blob of vagueness. It is actually the time when we shed our skin from the nature we are born into, to gaining awareness of what and whom we are. And what an agonizing process it is to find one's self!

Inbetweenness

The "in between" spell of adolescence will always stand out as a blur. If not for some radical yet indistinct feelings and thoughts that we have undergone, we might not be able to remember that period of life at all. We stumbled through paradise and inferno at the same time!

Time to Breathe

In the summer everything is as it supposed to be, fully grown, showing its true colors and form. It is a phase of auspicious comfort which seems will hold forever. Yet time flies by hastily in the busyness of warm days, and people forget to breathe.

The Crown of Life

I never knew I had a green thumb till I picked up gardening. Perhaps it is my blabbering that elicits a response in all plants. Perhaps it is my deep consideration of their divine roots that boasts their beauty. Perhaps it is that all life reacts to love the same, by budding profusely!

In the Moment

Moment

You know you are in a good place when you forget to yearn for a stage of life in past tense. Things are serene now. Nothing is missing, nothing at all. The stars are beaming above!

In Slow Motion

I would rather walk than fly. I want to witness how everything develops in slow motion, up close and personal. I want to reach, to touch, to hug. I have a choice in what to value or disregard. I have a choice in what to pursue and love or let go from my hands!

Native Place

I do not miss my native place, not anymore; a false discourse, of course. I cannot fall out of love with the nature that greeted me into this world in peace, with peace. It is not a memory to forget; it is not a mood or an impression to let pass by; it is my heritage, part of whom I am.

The Dirt I Am Made of

What is it about the place I was born that enthralls my heart? Is it the air or the landscape that links me to it, or the language, the culture, the archetypes that molded my young days? I am made of that dirt, thought to thought and limb to limb, up to the blood running through my veins.

Standpoint

I am walking on a waving path. From time to time I stop and look down the mountain. As I reach toward the top, the trees and the clouds give way to warm, caressing rays of sun. Close to the sky, far from insignificant daily matters, I cry joyful tears of gratefulness.

Humming Top

The days are warm and the skies blue most of the summer days. Yet in the overabundance of rich-green tones hides a tint of trite. People swirl like humming tops in all directions busy, too busy …

Kaleidoscope

Life is made of a few gems, just a few. All the nuances come from the angles, the mirrors, the lenses, the focus one looks through. Existence is as diverse and fascinating as the patterns in a kaleidoscope.

Contextual

Sometimes the skies look down upon us, unforgiving, and the sun displays a cold face as the heat sucks dry everything within its reach. Souls cry out for rain. Good and bad comes within the limits of a context!

Love a Child That Is Not Yours

Love a child that is not yours. Imprint hope in his heart. Be a strong branch for him to grab onto when the current pulls hard. Be a wholehearted being that goes beyond human prospects. Love the child that is not yours. Imprint hope in youths' hearts.

The Art of Life

Beauty means nothing without the moment of contemplation. The art of a life well lived is to capture flashes of beauty in random places. The wind blows softly at a lake on a summer afternoon. A stranger plays the guitar. Kids splash in the water. The sun shines just right!

The Moment in Which Beauty Is Seen

The moment in which beauty is seen, it grows even bigger from within. Sun's rays color the clouds even brighter, birds' songs seem more inviting, the wind feels so much more embracing. Meanings expand and slowly fade. We are here and now in the beauty we sense!

Through Life

From the peak of the mountain, a rock fell. Was chipped by rain, then rolled down by torrents; washed up by the waves of the ocean, emerged on the shore diminished, with all edges polished. We transform moving down the stream, yet inside we remain of the same essence!

In the Midst of Adversities

Given all conditions right, any tree grows with a full canopy, upright. Provided with a different setting, the tree will still grow, but crooked, as it bends to reach toward the light. Yet the most majestic tree of all is the one that raises its head tall in the harshest of adversities!

A Dewdrop's Gift

He saw the grass for the first time. Not that it wasn't near, but that he scurried each day by without care. He had to die dismantled, to learn how to be alive. A dewdrop on a green blade sparkled in the sun. At last, a glimpse he caught of heaven's gift and how beautiful it was!

Only One Side

Can empathy exist in a world without sorrow? No matter how unruffled, the sun grows callous after days and days of drought. Still, one can certainly be gentle without ever knowing harshness. After all, light does not hide a dark side in it!

Reflected in Our Eyes

A blue moon was shining upon us. Perhaps it had nothing special to it, not even a blue tint, unless one really stretched one's mind to envision it. The extraordinary side of everything in this universe lies in their presence and, more so, in our acknowledgement of such presence.

Light's Reflection on Our Heart

The moon gleams in its fullness when nothing hinders sun's rays. The same, man shines in his richness when he rests in full light. A crescent moon is still as lovely but a man lurking in mud is utterly ugly. The moon's movement is a given but man can choose his position freely.

Peaceful Summer Nights

Oh, how I will miss the summer nights with fireflies; the crickets playing their chords and the frogs, their trombones; the stars in distance smiling kindly and a fresh breeze descending gently! I close my eyes and fall asleep as peaceful as a full blue moon in a cloudless ether.

The Potentiality of Dawn

Oh, how I will miss the summer mornings with all the chatter and the cheeping and the scurrying and the flutter—such liveliness from every corner of every bush and every tree! Through a gateway of potentiality, the light of dawn is smiling warmly!

The Forest Within

In the heat of a summer's day, find a moment to stand still like a tree. In tranquility, you will hear the heart of life beating within and outside you. Every cell is as much alive as every leaf in every tree, and every bird, and every other earthly creature—and all fulfill a worthy purpose.

In the Hassle of a Week's Work

After a week's work, the world comes to a halt. The tension we carried all along is melting away and after a short reflection, the significance of the worry, the rush, and the hassle dwindles. Too close, too attached, we lose perspective of what is relevant: the one butterfly passing by.

Attention to Details

First a black butterfly with an intricate blue, white, and red design on the edges fluttered by, then a yellow one followed. When the third zigzagged around me again and again, I knew the universe was talking to me. My time of metamorphosis, of transcendence, had come. I believe!

The Dream Born to You

The clearer a dream becomes, the more likely it is to materialize. Push on, don't let the momentum go. It is easier to float on the air currents above than to rise from the ground each time. Push on… Only the dream that you are meant to fulfill is born to you. Push on…

Fully Charged Universe

Infinity above and infinity within; larger and larger forever and smaller and smaller till matter becomes just a spark and further on, more like nothing than something, a simple potentiality. Ideas are the same; they can come into existence or not. Our universe is fully charged!

As Above, the Same Below

The mind is but a medium; it is what transpires in us. Yet the human spirit is not in the mind. The human spirit is in our every cell. Born to a spark, it emerges in our body fully formed. Seemingly minor, the heart is its true hub, like a sun around which everything else revolves.

Living Proof

We are the living proof that, in this universe, there is something else besides the matter we can observe and dissect; something we cannot perceive with our limited physical eyesight nor envision with our biased minds. Besides, what matters the most to us was never material!

Reoccurrence

Overnight, at a precise time yet, sneaking out on us, the summer day started to shorten. Everything has a crescendo, an apex, and a decline stage; from the pit, another loop will start. As long as beings find within the power to raise and push through a new cycle, life will move on.

The Mammoth Tree

The mammoth tree rises above everything else, as a highlight of endurance and wits, with many bruises, hollows, and lacerations, but also with many stories to tell. The same, our mammoth elders lead the way for us to follow their steps into a well-lived life, to a natural end.

Letter from the Prison of Societal Norms

Imprisoned, I learned to look up at the ceiling and see the clouds through them. Edifying books were forbidden, but I listened to the stories told by the wind. Although my hands were chained, my spirit soared free to the highest transcendental realms.

A Change of Discourse

Society manages to survive through norms. No matter how much those norms change, and what direction they take, in the end they are still limiting. In any society man fights to live on. Perhaps it is exactly this survival mode of thinking that keeps us from truly evolving!

Passing through Utopia

I refused to learn what communism meant or what it was standing for. I was living it. It was wrong beyond any philosophical theory—a utopian fallacy that brought only ruins and devastation. For a better world to exist, our human nature needs to transmute!

Hope for Another Day

People die fighting for a rightful cause when they can endure no more. Behind curtains, the politics of this world are decided to favor the powerful men of the times. A morsel will be returned to them, the people below… They will rise again when they can endure no more.

When the Dam Shatters

In revolt, a tumultuous downpour of humans was coming down the main street, gushing with force. I joined in—a drop of water in an immensity of mental and emotional wretchedness. People act in spite of dangers when they can endure no more!

A Facade

I was not killed that day of insurrection while many others were. The red flag went down in blood with the communist political façade. Another system took its place. Passing over a historical landmark, people went on living. All seems forgotten now. Other problems followed…

A Square World

Every day, dressed in a uniform, I walked by square communist flats looking like matchboxes. In another square building, my school, I sat down in a square desk and read square books. We are guided by square laws and live in square enclosures as we keep our mind sealed in a square.

The Gray of Our Souls

The gray was killing my soul, gray roads, faces, feelings, and thoughts… When the communist crest fell, another shade of gray transpired, as pervasive. It is the gray of our own limiting nature regardless of the square we live in. As humanity, we do not know how to soar above!

The Communist Tsunami

No regime is bad across all places, situations, times, or populations. The tsunami wave hits the hardest at its breaking point. Caught in the middle of such a crashing force, I and what I stood for, tore apart. It was the timing of my birth and growth. There is no point to regret…

Part of History

Days roll in like waves on the ocean. Societal changes make the humankind mass rise and fall with the tide. Once in a while, the winds and the pressure trigger immense storm surges. Caught in the middle of such a crashing force, one becomes part of history.

The First Breath

Out the window, I could see the morning sun rising behind the mountains. The rest doesn't matter because that soft and playful light and the peaks on the horizon were engraved in my heart with my first breath. Vast zeniths grew within me since, with tender light shining amidst.

Going Home

I do not need a reason to want to climb a mountain, as it is not I but the mountain itself that calls me. I am not stepping on a path for what I want to become, but for what I am. Up on open heights, where Heaven and Earth merge, lies my spiritual dwelling. I am going home!

Parenting Mistakes

Perhaps nothing is as painful to live with as are our faults as parents. They are the most hurtful not because of a malice in our acts, but because the wounded ones are so young, defenseless, and fully dependent on us. We are the sun to them and sometimes we burn their little hearts!

Abandoning My Child

I abandoned my child. I abandoned my child for the American Dream. After years have passed, I saw the damage I have caused in him and in me. Guilt ate my insides through years to come; it carried on an inconsolable pain for both of us. Forgive me, my child, for I have wronged you!

Surviving through the First Tempest

No child emerges from infancy unbruised and no youngster from the adolescent years, unbowed. No one can escape life's setbacks without unbearable, felt agony. On the other side of the first tempest is not brighter; but we surface better equipped to withstand any storm.

The Human Condition 1

What is it that we learn about ourselves and the world during our teenage years that crushes us to pieces? Injustice, discrimination, cruelty... and the alienation of the man within society. Somehow, we patch up ourselves and numb that which we should never forget!

The Human Condition 2

The world will not change after a tempest. More distant we are befalling with each, more numb and closed up. We let the injustice, discrimination, cruelty, and the alienation of the human within society pass by. By doing so, we become part of it, preserving that which hurt us...

The Human Condition 3

We are conflicted between what we aspire for and what is. We aim for peace, yet we do nothing to achieve it. We long for love, yet we fail to live by it. Our reality is a reflection of our inaction and disinterest. We, ourselves, are not what we are asking from and of the world!

Only in Two

From time to time, the urge of loving and to be loved stirs my inside waters. A storm impinges upon my soul and I cannot but be a helpless bystander, petrified of the intense lightning that strikes close to my heart. Drenched, I dare to believe that love will eventually find me.

Hidden Nakedness 1

Like Adam and Eve, we hide our naked inner selves, afraid… afraid of our own failures and imperfections, afraid of becoming exposed and diminished. Yet understanding the circumstances and genuineness of our failures and imperfections makes us humane!

Hidden Nakedness 2

Like Eve and Adam, we tend to hide our naked inner selves, filled with sorrow and remorsefulness. Yet holding shame and guilt in is by far more alienating and painful than the nakedness itself. We fall apart in a dry land of isolation where it never rains.

Hidden Nakedness 3

Like Eve and Adam, we taste from the apple of knowledge. What we are becoming aware of cannot be undone. At the most, we can hold onto the innocence of our expanding mindfulness. Liberated, we find ourselves naked in the face of the universe, naked…

Adam and Eve

Adam and Eve did not ask for help or for forgiveness after eating the forbidden fruit. Baffled, my mind pauses. I have nothing more to say although many "if" and "what if" queries flood my mind. Sometimes realities are given to us in the form of tacit assumptions.

The Human Factor

Set time to ponder about the source of your actions and reactions. We can play out our inner preconceptions, respond to external provocations, or mix drives together. The dance among us, with giving and taking, is what determines the direction and the strength of our relationships.

With a Sharing Heart

Why Abel was favored versus Cain does not transpire from their deeds. Hidden purity, unseen to the naked eye, is what truly counted. A benefactor picks the recipient that elicits his bestowment. In spite of one's acts, it is the untainted heart that makes all the difference!

I and the Deer

I step in silence on my lawn with bare feet at times, while the moon is shining among stars. The grass feels soft and wet from the night's dewdrops. The green blades bow under each stride I take. Erstwhile we meet our eyes, me and a deer, both surprised. The life in us is one.

Summer Storms

Fascinating… summer storm clouds develop out of the blue, emerging one from another… faraway lightning strikes nearer and nearer… the wind closes in, hisses and huffs, announcing its imminence. And then it pours in short, heavy bursts till the clouds dissipate in nothingness…

Relationship Twisters

Summer storms are coming fast, voice piercingly, and leave as if they were never here. Once in a while the conditions are wrong, and opposing currents of air funnel a twister. Whatever was before is shattered down to the ground. Broken, people part their ways…

Life's Poesy

Outwardly, modern humans show displeasure for verses; internally, is what all are in search of. Come rain or shine, life's poesy is what brings us hope, inspiration, and joy. I am standing for this touchy-feely concept nobody cares about, yet everybody longs for!

Disclaimer

I do not write about an objective, whole truth that occurs outside my existence. I expose relative views in their naked form, from where I stand at each moment. Sometimes, I look at the world sideways or upside down. Not to be right but to stir thought is my only purpose.

Fata Morgana

The American Dream is a *Fata Morgana*, alluring lost travelers. The life conditions provoke illusory perceptions of wealth and achievement, in a seemingly inverted social structure. Not all is a mirage, but what one sees in the distance is not what one will find close up.

The Trail of Wailing Sorrows

The refugees are coming. Only they know the ailments they are fleeing from; we all know, though, what are they fleeing for. The refugees march on a trail of wailing sorrows, hanging on a thread of hope. Like migratory birds, many of them will perish on a road without return.

The Symphony of Life

The Symphony of Life

It was just me and countless stars, in a summer night without moon. Eons they persist in the skies, while I on Earth, a mere moment. Gleaming, they enchant my eyes; to them, I am a nonentity. The crickets' symphony though, it is I who listens closely.

Selective Point of View

We select what to hear, we select what to see, we tune out overflowing emotions, and we bury unwanted thoughts in bottomless pits. We withhold being in action and so often, we deny love. Withdrawn in our world, we wonder why our life is so lonely and meaningless.

The Life-Giving Tree

Knowledge is freeing. The more you know, the more you understand the human world and the more you are able to rise above day-to-day worries. Knowledge is binding. The more you know, the more responsible you are to grow and stand tall, a life-giving tree.

High-Spirited Fiddles

A gust of autumn descended all of a sudden. The crickets don't know it as of yet. They continue to play their fiddles as spirited as they did in their prime days. Why are we humans holding back, I wonder, from living in the now in our fullness, giving it all, burning alive?

The Owl

I was awakened in the middle of the night by a prey's plea for life and an owl's hooting as it answered back. The meaning I found after days of deep soul searches. The victim challenged the sage, both within me. In the end, in the struggle for survival, the owl stood its ground!

Defeating Predeterminations

Each tree blossoms at its time—predetermined within its specie, some in early spring and some in late fall—and each will ripen at its time. What is predetermined is subjected to shifts in winds. Once in a while, a tree's will to flourish is stronger than the odds against it.

Breaking Wave

"Oh, Ocean," I sigh, "how important is it for one to manifest her own call?" The waves are breaking in white bubbles. I did not reach that height, the point where the crest of my being overturns and starts spilling forward toward the shores of my imagination, in a crushing plunge!

Adornments

Life is made up of moments; those moments are as special as one elects them to be. The same waves and clouds, shells, and butterflies pass by everyone indiscriminately. The eye looks at them with fear, disdain, indifference, or wonder. Each choice colors one's life!

Finding Direction

One finds in life what one is looking for. Some random happenings might come and go. We might chase random matters for random reasons. Most of the time we fret, restless, lacking the awareness of our true longing. But once we know it, we turn in the right direction…

An Angel with a Broken Wing

Like an angel with a broken wing, I can neither fly nor walk straight. Limping, I drag my wing on the muddy side of the road while I dream to soar high. I try to hide the wing; all it does is to magnify the contrast between what I am and what I have to live with.

By the Shore

We hang out in shallow waters, where we know what we see. But a true journey starts in the deeps, where everything is indistinct. What works or doesn't, we learn as we venture into the unfamiliar. No matter the perils, the ache is more tormenting from up the shore.

Rotting from Inside

We are keen on washing our body every day, but we do not put forth the same effort to clean our heart. Dust clusters in corners; then mold creeps in. Feelings we refused to deal with, to set right, to set free, start to decay. When it smells so bad we cannot breathe, we cry...

Beyond a Ceiling

With wings from wax and feathers, Icarus proceeded in his voyage. "Keep your fly neither low nor high," his father urged. The sun's glimmer enticed Icarus. Close to the atmospheric limits, his wings did not melt but froze. Only so far a human can rise before tumbling from the skies!

Undying Myths

The myth's testimonial is undying. It gives a name to each human challenge and pursuit, trap and pitfall, breakdown and breakthrough. The society itself appears with faces of monsters but most of the time, the creatures are within us, ready to strike!

Songs of a Different Tone

As clouds close in or draw apart, poems soar in my mind—birds of a different feather—barging in from my past. Their songs are in a language I don't speak anymore; though, their tone soothes my soul. There is no one to share them with, only the wind, only the wind…

Magnified Glitches

Adults are children with magnified glitches. Their original qualms expand in a hunchback. Its weight thrusts them down, facing the mud. But from knees they can still rise, like sprouts pushing on through the shadow of difficulties, toward the warm rays of sun.

Interconnectedness in the Material Realm

One single match can burn down a forest. A storm brings rain and flooding from one end of the world to another. In spite of undeniable evidence, we choose to live in oblivion. Like ripples on the surface of the water, the effect of any event will eventually reach all of us!

Interconnectedness in the Social Realm

One single match can burn down a forest. One single emotion or thought can change one's state of mind. A riot starts with one. People's views and feelings added together move the social mass. In the flow of the current, each individual is either dragged in or pushed out.

Interconnectedness in the Spiritual Realm

One single match can burn down a forest. But what one prayer does remains covered. Unseen and unvalued, based on the elusive hope and belief, coming together as one, brings to our world peace. On the spiritual realm, love and kindness unite us!

Defiance

And if this day you can't get up, pull even more, just in spite! Moment by moment that you can't but in defiance, do, shapes the champion in you. And perhaps, just perhaps, in one such moment you will bloom, in spite of odds, just in spite!

Torment

I cannot escape my fate. The call since my birth, the dreams of my youth, didn't go away, but deepened with time. In torment, they hunted me down night and day. Tormented, I ran. Now, I choose to stay!

Frail Corner

Scared we are of the pain of living and loving, but feeling nothing, petrifies us even more. From our dim corner, we look up at the sky. We spot among clouds the white trace of a passing plane that carries on people like us, insecure and frail, as terrified of life as they are of death.

With a Perfect Soul 1

Each of us is a perfect soul in an imperfect body. Our corporeal form sways our ability to fully manifest our true form. Any illness and ailment, any chemical imbalance or genetic misprint, disturbs the divine being that dwells within.

With a Perfect Soul 2

Each of us is a perfect soul in an imperfect body. Sometimes, a being is so deeply buried inside that what is seen carries no resemblance with the divine. The very inner landscape is under siege; nothing can come out, nothing can get in!

With a Perfect Soul 3

Each of us is a perfect soul in an imperfect body. Our materiality, with its biological makeup, its needs, its social and physical exchanges with the world, confines us. In the midst of all predeterminations, how we use our heart is our choice!

Determined Stand

Everything that happens in one's life influences one's stand. For the same occurrence though, different people have different responses as what happens in each one's life goes through different filters and lenses. As long as one is aware of this bias, one is not slave to one's past.

Undetermined Stand

Everything that happens in one's life influences one's stand. Yet the true determining factor comes to us from before our birth. No matter what life throws at us, the call remains immutable, beyond personal filters and lenses. It is the spiritual imprint of our true being!

Afflictions 1

Dreading I might find out I am what I believe I am, I waved. Chances went by, one by one. I remained hidden, in shame. I let myself down, crushed, agonizing, and depressed. The belief grew stronger. So did the fear. Doubt is a dreadful plague, hard to overcome.

Afflictions 2

My demons are strong, dark, and voracious. They feed on my doubts, on my insecurities, on my qualms. They are hungry the most for my shame. I am ashamed for believing there is greatness in me. I am ashamed for yearning to be what I believe I am.

Afflictions 3

And when I am in acute pain, when desperation grows so overwhelming it pushes me over the edge, I remember that the greatness I feel in me is a gift, not mine to keep hidden, to doubt, to be ashamed of. It is a gift meant to be passed on, holding nothing back!

Dulce-Lacrimosa 1 (Sweet-Weeping)

What a symphony life is! *Andante* at times, at others, *allegro*; piano under the moonlight, but with *forte* affairs and tensions; so *dolce* and dreamy yet with *lacrimato* spells and downfalls. Each life plays in the air, in a unique tune, till its last breath.

Dulce-Lacrimosa 2

What a symphony life is! From afar looks like an explosion of constellations, expanding through the skies. Over a microscope, each cell seems to influence the others into a domino befall. But from one's shoes, life is a continuous weeping, sweet at times, very sweet...

Dulce-Lacrimosa 3

What a symphony life is! During each movement, with its dynamics and rhythms, we spill many tears and find many likes. The allegorical expression, carries us on a stream of dreams. The most poignant symphony of all is orchestrated and played with an open soul!

Out of the Ordinary

Four planets were aligned in the morning sky; they looked like any other stars. One wouldn't prize their display unless one would know how singular they are. Many opportunities in life look like distant stars as well. One wouldn't see them unless one would know how singular they are!

Nothingness

Everything will disappear in nothingness sooner or later. Yet we hold tight onto pursuing one goal after another and another, stressing over attainments that do not matter. We cling with desperation as if letting go will make us tumble in the nothingness we fear of.

A Moment of Possibilities

The solitary hanging nail vanished with all the possibilities it stood for. Now it is a hole, in the place of a nail, on a wall. Soon, even the memory would be gone as if the nail wasn't there at all. As illusory our life is. But for a moment, it embodies all possibilities!

The Portal Within

She was born today—after dozens of years of pain and latency—into the prospect of fulfillment and happiness. Perhaps a portal unlocked in front of her, or perhaps it was her opening up to a portal that was always there! Though fearful, she chose to step forward.

Step Forward

She chose to step forward when the fear of what is, stood greater than the fear of what can be. The risk looked less risky than not taking the risk. Not trying become crushingly prominent. And time was not on her side anymore.

The Path of Butterflies

Although troubled by the immensity of "what if" doubts, she knew there is no other way to stay alive inside but by following the path of butterflies—her ideas, and hopes, and dreams. Acknowledgment of what life is and where she stands became her ally.

Toward the Blue Skies

"Do I deserve fulfillment and happiness?" she wondered under the frown of gray clouds. "Can I hope to see the blue skies one day?" The azure smiled, "I am always here above veils, omnipresent. I am the portal." Though fearful, she chose to step forward.

The Dance of Life

And if the days are like leaves, falling one by one, then I want to be an oak tree, with foliage holding strong on branches, holding strong far into the winter. And if the leaves are like days, I want to see them drop in full colors, dancing…

The Day of the Dead

The Day of the Dead comes after the crops have been harvested. We remember what was and lament over the impermanence of our own life and youthful love. Hiding behind a mask, we put that which has passed to rest and give way to renewal.

Testimony of Life

The leaves are falling and with them are tumbling poems after poems.
They spin in the air for a moment, free from any material purpose.
The ground is their graveyard—yet a testimony of the fullness of life.

In a Renaissance Spring

If everything moves in circles, then the time of poetry will come back one day. For now, the verses lie dormant under the fallen leaves soaking in the pain of the world, the cries of dying nature, the lost songs of love … They will sprout again in a Renaissance spring.

An Embrace

I miss being in someone's arms, feeling safe, with each worry gone.
I miss being in someone's arms, hearing another heart beating by mine.
I miss being in someone's arms, utterly vulnerable, with all defenses shut down.

Vibrations

By myself I am neutral and balanced. But sometimes, I wish I am not by myself;
I wish that my impartiality would become polarized, vibrating in different patterns
of highs and lows. Sometimes I long to be alive—a liveliness that only love can inspire!

Never-Ending Springs

There is a hidden place of never-ending springs, where winds blow gently, and joy flows freely.
There is a hidden place in one's heart, a fountain of fresh water that never gets dry.
It is the place where inspiration comes from, blooming and flowering, gushing out love!

Out of Balance

Don't be afraid to fall out of balance. This is how new beginnings start, with a thrust,
by mistake. The whole dance of creation lies in the plunge itself. Everything
in and out moves in a divergent fashion. The unexpected becomes exposed!

The Unexpected

The unexpected becomes exposed as you look at the world from a different angle, with a different eye, from a different place. All of a sudden you can see what lies between lines and beyond ends. The windows of your heart are open wide!

Open Your Windows

Open the windows of your heart; let the unexpected surprise you.
It will come in the form of butterflies with diaphanous reveries and drops of morning dew reflecting hope. Let yourself fall out of balance, plunge in...

A Patterned World

We are made to distinguish patterns, the regularity of lines, shapes, sounds, thoughts...
Our brain reacts abruptly to disruptions in rhythms. From inert, our instinct of survival and our awareness rekindles. Awake, we burn in flames for a little while...

A Break in Pattern

We are made to distinguish patterns. As soon as we perceive a dissonance, we awaken from a slumber state of automatic functioning. Disharmony elicits a frantic search for a cause. We rationalize our motive and adopt a solution that allows us to fall back into mindless apathy.

The Thread That Holds Us

We are made to distinguish patterns. We are made to search for meaning, to make sense of the inexplicable. As one rationale ends, we strain to catch onto another thread. Without a belief to hold onto, anxiety conquers our heart, and we fall adrift into a vast chasm.

Through the Eye of an Artist

We are made to distinguish patterns. Artists are inclined even more so to be deeply affected by naturally occurring configurations as well as by their absence, for they live on a higher plane of vibration. Their intense storms of thoughts and feelings are turned into art!

In Search for Imponderability

We are made to distinguish patterns. Only love comes sneaking on, patternless. It sweeps us away off our feet, in a free flight. When in love, no canons, no structures, no orderliness restricts or grounds us anymore. Love plays by no rules!

A Stormy Sea

Countless times my life I started over. I hoped I would have learned how to sail across the sea; that over calm waters I would stumble. I discovered instead beauty in a gloomy sky and on endless days of rains and winds. For traveler, you see, calm waters get you nowhere!

Turning the Page

I am turning one more page. I am afraid to look forward with joy for I know that each page gets me closer to the end of my book. And I did not learn all that I wanted to. And I did not reach the heights I dreamed of. And I did not love enough …

The Symphony of My Life

I am dying, today or maybe the day after an unknown tomorrow. Since I know I am dying, why not focus on living, living all that I want to live, without restraints? It is the symphony of my life that I listen to and that I write at the same time. It is my symphony of life!

Untainted

Like a spectacular fall, I want to go out bursting in flames with all leaves and sky fiery intense. I have in me that dream and so, I should have the power to make it stand. The aim was born to me, maybe not perfect, but perfectly untainted!

Farewell

Herds of leaves were shepherded by the wind; rolled down the streets, stopped, and then rolled again on another gust. They are troubadours of our souls—feelings and dreams that bloomed when time was young. "Adios," I'd say, "you served life well!"

Tryptics

A Colorful Universe 1

I had to stretch my mind, to let images distort and entangle till they adjusted into something intelligible. Only then I was able to distinguish the blue ones. They are quiet and walk alone. An echo of clear skies and tranquil waters, they are radiating peace and calmness.

A Colorful Universe 2

Bursting in flames are the red folks, full of excitement and resilience. Always on the move, from the land of the sun and scorching fire, they are born on Earth to inspire. Along travels the green family. Their compassion embodies the essence of the true human nature.

A Colorful Universe 3

We live in a colorful universe yet we describe people in black-and-white terms. Our mind perceives what we let ourselves see, what everyone else points out to, what is engraved in our ways. We choose what we reflect. Souls arrive in this world as light—free of judgment!

The Third World War 1

So easily we forgot the lessons of our past, with all the pains and losses, to put ourselves on the brink of another world war. A conflict is started by the evilness of few and spreads like fire in a dry land. In the end, all children will suffer for the mistakes of their parents!

The Third World War 2

In the end, all children will suffer for the mistakes of their parents! History attests again and again that no descendant of the wicked was ever spared. There is no safe haven for them. The blood will ask for blood, and blood will be spilled till there is nothing more to be upheld.

The Third World War 3

And blood will be spilled till there is nothing more to be upheld. No one neighbor would be left with something of value to covet, other than tears and hurt. An empty Earth will surface free of people and their vile ways. All the children would have died by then, all of them …

Let Go

She went by the edge of the river and set them free, on paper boats, memory by memory… She smiled as she let go of each of them, picture after picture. "Farewell, illusions, farewell! You will not hold me back anymore, for I am letting you be what you are—artifacts of the past!"

Artifacts of the Past

Each boat, with each picture—artifacts of the past—followed the current of the water. As they passed on, one by one, their potency diminished and the holding bond became thinner and thinner till it broke. "Farewell, illusions, farewell! You will not define my life anymore!"

Freeing a New Path

Letting go to what holds you back in the past frees the way for a future that you can own; unrestricted by preconceptions, by intents without actions, by dreams that you set aside for a right moment that can be never right. It is time to take charge of your life and persist…

Lacking Essence

We are missing what should define our essence: Humanity! Without this essence, we turn into the opposite—being inhumane. Even the concrete is weeping its impending doom as we are as pitiless of the inanimate entities as we are of the animated ones. Each has a full life to live!

Lacking Humanity

The world is crying out for Humanity! Yet who is to give humans humanity? The trees grow flowers and leaves, and the birds nurture their flying wings; only humans don't strive to advance what is uniquely theirs, as if their well-being and identity and lives do not depend on it!

Longing for Humanity

In what corner of our heart lies Humanity? So high we built the walls around our true nature that joy cannot reach in, or the light of hope, or the warmth of love! We long with all our being for that which we withhold—HUMANITY. And humanity cries, locked in a corner of our heart!

Life's Quandaries

Each life has a story to tell, a story of quandaries and dearth, toil and unrest. It is a story of determination to survive, to stand, to be… We get up each morning and worry, fight with each drawback, fall, and sometimes land ahead, get up the next morning, get up…

Life's Nectar

Each life has a story to tell, a story of triumphs. We become victors each time we get up from our knees. We are victors over times of lamentation, of helplessness, of desperation. Privations get the better years of us, our flowers too, yet for a little bit of nectar, we push forward!

Life's Yearning

Each life has a story to tell, a story of love. Bashful, we search in earnest for the one that perfects us. We walk a twisty path of trials with irresistible airs luring us, both sweet and sad. We remain true to our hunger for the kiss, caresses, and romance that makes us feel complete.

A Dried Spring

Several days have passed and I wrote nothing. The creative flow has stopped and the spring of imagination has dried out. Without my joyous reveries, I feel scared and lost. The sky is gloomy, the birds are silent, the leaves are fallen, and I don't know what direction to take…

A Single Stroke

I have nothing to say, yet I decided to scrawl about having nothing to say. Indecisive, I drag the brush onto the empty canvas. I am painting nothing yet, the very stroke forced the nothingness to become a possibility. This is all that it takes to make a change—a single thrust!

Downtime of Reflection

The hollowness of the white page called me, and words that I do not have to say poured out! They talk about the void that we all feel at times. We crawl into a fetus position, and germinate, gathering strength to reemerge. The downtime of reflection revives our inner strings.

Life Moves On 1

Life moves on. We live or we die, create or ignore our call, take action or let it go. No matter what we choose, life moves on. Other people will live, will create, will take action, and in the end will die just like us, as if nothing mattered, neither pain, nor love!

Life Moves On 2

Life moves on. I want to see each tomorrow with hope anew, witnessing dreams blooming. I want to be unafraid of what comes next, for by then, I would have lived my life and loved wholly, in all respects. Life moves on…

Life Moves On 3

Everywhere I look, life moves on—the nests that wait for the spring to come by again and a new generation of youngsters kissing in hidden corners. Only I am stuck in a memory of a love that never existed. I only wish I had the strength to let my inner life move on as well!

What Was, What Is 1

Nobody told me I was beautiful, or perhaps many did, but I had no ears to listen. Time had passed and all that beauty remained forgotten in a frame. Now I can see it clearly, but the beautiful one is gone. Only the light in my eyes is the same, only the light…

What Was, What Is 2

Nobody told me I was smart and talented, or perhaps many did, but I had no ears to listen. As chances went by empty handed, I understood late in life that creative ideas do not matter unless they are put to good use. Now I stand up and fight to overcome drawbacks, now I stand!

What Was, What Is 3

People told me my heart is good, but I had no ears to listen their advice and act with caution. I dove in headfirst! I thought I have unlimited strength till one day, when my heart broke in half. Held together by stitches, pulses the same, pure and childish, still believing in beauty and love!

Meanings in the Sky

Creativity appears like rays of sun amid clouds, through a window of opportunity. You can never be fully prepared, for creativity descends on its own when the conditions are right. Many bystanders see the rays of sun, but only some can capture a message!

The Inexpressible

Creativity comes in many forms. It can be a simple addition to what is known. It can show up as a reincarnation of experiences, feelings, and thoughts. It can emerge all of a sudden as a new, intergalactic star. To express the inexpressible is the most unique way of creation of all.

A Fallen Angel

Creativity glows with excitement and wonderment. One's spirit transcends to another plane of vibration away from the material here and now. Returning to the quotidian—a fallen angel—hurts. The burden of living in dirt, amid humans, full of worries and cries, becomes pervasive.

Return to Nothingness

There is not even a grain of sand in the nothingness's desert. No side is up or down, east or west—all is nowhere, without a point of reference. She feels nothing, no happiness nor pain, no desires nor sorrows, only detachment. Yesterday will be in the tomorrow that left already.

Inescapable Nothingness

Her world is completely empty. With closed eyes or opened, all is the same—inescapable void. There is no reflection, only dense, insubstantial opaque. No rustles, or whispers, or singing befalls, only silence transpires from immaterial walls. And nothing is life, and death is nothing.

Indefinite Nothingness

Looking at it from afar, with a very cold eye, I see nothing more than a crescent moon on an icy, distant sky—a simple object without meaning. The beauty I used to see died from my imagination. Indefinite nothingness invaded me. In this empty void, freezing, I quiver.

Buried Potentiality

Letting go to presumptions opens a portal of opportunity in the spiritual world. Things will start to happen, materializing into objective reality. The acorn did nothing more than let itself fall. Under leaves it stays still till warm rays of sun call for it to raise to its dormant potentiality.

The Wishless List

Perhaps it is the lack of expectations that gives way to the unexpected to occur. Looking for a chance closes the door to the unintended. To reach the Ocean, the stream of passion has to flow freely. Any wish, any anticipation of outcomes, restricts and delays its natural course.

Low Point

What a relief to lack any trace of yearning, at times, for without desire neither does fear exist; without dread, no urgency has a hold on our soul, and without worries, no doubts are left to pin us down. Quietness lingers before the wheel starts off into a new, wandering cycle!

Pretense

So many wants we have in life, and yet so little we pursue. So many longings and needs troubles us, yet what we attempt is but insignificant. We settle too soon, get complacent, survive the day under the pretense that we have tried hard enough…

Crumbles

So little we accomplish, and perhaps for what we dream is crumbles. We fail to commit to love and to create, to discover, to take a stand. Each minute calls for our action, yet so little we ask of ourselves, so low we aim, so fast and easily we give up!

The Grain of Mustard

What is it that I want from me today, to be, to do, to find, to see? I have nothing in mind, nothing at all. My dreams, my aim, my will to yearn is smaller than a grain of mustard. I have power within me to move mountains, yet I fail to commit, I fail to put forth the effort!

Toward the Sunset

From seventeen to forty-seven, so many things have changed, and yet so few. I feel lost like then, as insecure and unformed. I know who I am no more than I knew when life was at its dawn. Nonetheless now, as I walk toward the sunset, I see in the distance love stories flying freely.

Life's Elusory Nature

From seventeen to forty-seven, so many things I did and yet so few. Rhymes I noted here and there about love, but love itself eluded me. After so many years, affection remains a phantasm still. My deepest sorrow is not life's elusory nature, but the many verses I did not print.

Filling into My Shoes

From seventeen to forty-seven, I stayed the same—only appearances are tarnished. I might have grown to be the one elder who guides and stirs young souls into becoming divine beings with a purpose on Earth. I might have finally agreed to fill into my own shoes and dance!

Cupid's Whim

Cupid smiled at me behind a ray of sun descending gently on the mortal world because he knew that what I am looking for is not up to me, but to his whim. "Well, strike me," I yelled, from the top of my lungs. "What more do you want? Haven't I waited long enough for love?"

Unforeseen Butterfly

"Love is not up to you," Cupid confessed with candor. "It is indeed like a butterfly, full of charm and colors, but it dissipates into the light when you close your hand to catch its splendor. You should not wait for love, for it comes on its own will, at an unforeseen moment!"

The Gust of Love

I yearned to reach for the stars immersed in fiery passion. Inspired by the spark of love, I would have soared high on a warm gust of intimate affection. "I waited long enough for true love," I cried. "No," Cupid said, leveling his arrow. "You never opened your heart!"

Going Further

Going further in one's imagination or going further in the universe—it never ends, it is never the same, yet the laws that hold everything together are unchanged. An infinity of possibilities exist, still only one comes into being. Each of us beat that odd, each one of us!

Algorithms

Precise mathematical algorithms keep matters in balance, or so we think, as if reality conforms to an underlying Fibonacci sequence or other such particularities. Once in a while, one visionary eye reads between lines and makes a leap of faith into new knowledge!

All Is Old

All is old. New can be found only in our awareness of all that is since the beginning of the world. What we are sentient of is limited to our immediate needs and wants and surroundings. Our own mind is a universe, yet we are afraid to explore possibilities!

Outsider

When I am reminded of my birthplace, a sudden ache pierces my heart. I did not know what I had, how precious it was to me—the ground under my feet, the air in my lungs, and the hopes in my dreams! I am an outsider in this life, on a cold and foreign land.

Romantic Chants of a Lost Tongue

When I am reminded of my mother tongue, a sudden ache pierces my heart. I did not know what I had, how precious it was to me—words that depict a particular meaning in my mind, an ancient language with romantic chants, soothing, touching… Nothing on Earth is alike!

Above Clouds

When melancholy is intruding all chambers of my being, I let my spirit fly back to my native land. Seraphs escort me into the clouds. Familiar psalms are lifting the dark veils of everyday doubts. The magic of life shows its face once more. I remember how blessed I am!

Oneness 1

My home is on the highest plateau of a mountain, where earth and heavens meet in the clouds and shepherds travel freely on unmarked paths, amid timeless pillars. Up there, in quietness, by petite, diaphanous flowers and grass bowing in the wind, I am one with the whole universe!

Oneness 2

The forest is my shrine. Moss and ferns grow on me slowly as I expand into a tree. The rustle of the leaves, the chirping of the birds, the murmur of fresh springs caresses my being. The woods reconnect me with life and replenish my will to move forward. I and the nature are one!

Oneness 3

When my being is overridden by pain, I go by the Ocean to cleanse. I cry loudly and throw a fit, lamenting over life's disillusions, failures, and sorrows. The waves listen and listen and finally silence me. "Hush, human, hush. I'll take your worries for now. Make peace with yourself!"

Social Cohesion

Life amidst humans is about following the laws of the social structure. We are all ants in an anthill, working our way mindlessly toward our own demise. Each of us, although unique, is replaceable. The society as a whole stays cohesive regardless of each person's individuality.

Coexistence

Life amidst humans is about fitting into a particular place, with leaders, fellows, and family nests. Each tribe has habits and customs that keep a community's sense of closeness. Traditions help us coexist and cope with life's hardships through sharing our familiar joys and suffering.

Individual Distinction

Life in a body reduces our existence to an individual struggle for survival. All emotions, needs, searches, cannot be but intrinsically personal. As a distinct entity, we cannot escape separateness. Yet here is where we err. Giving does not take away from our wealth; rather, it enriches it!

Beautiful by Design

The human being is a fascinating entity. Every little detail has a perfect design. Nothing is made more or less of, but just right to be highly proficient for life on Earth. Our eyes are an individually cut kaleidoscope in which the whole world is reflected. Each one of us is a remarkable universe!

Beautiful by Choice

The human being is a fascinating entity. From close up, however, the human shows a lot of murkiness. Although perfect by nature, he can soil his flawlessness by the choices he makes. Feeble yet potent, he controls his soul's path toward being oppressive or forgiving and loving.

Beautiful in Love

I adore flowers, yet people fascinate me even more so. If I count petals and notice the wildlife's harmony, I see impeccability in humans even more so. Living in nature is serene and joyous, but amidst people is rough. With all the blooms in the world, it is a human heart I long the most for!

Voices of the Past

We all have a past that holds us prisoner. Ancient judgments and disapproval follow our steps like a shadow, reminding us how insignificant we felt. Instinctively, we jerk back in fear. As long as one holds true the voices of the past, one cannot escape one's own confinement!

Confinement

We all have a past that holds us prisoner. No accomplishment seems to matter when one tallies one's failures. Without the risk for breakdowns, breakthroughs are not possible. As long as one clenches onto a safety zone, one cannot escape confinement and fly freely!

Unshackled

Perhaps it was I who kept the past hostage, for it was easier to blame bygones than to stand on my feet. As I opened the door of the prison, the chains that held me down unshackled. Unconfined by fears from the past, I can work on my visions. The power is always in us!

The Blissful Feminine

Sameness

Each morning, I am drinking hot chocolate with the spirit of my father, the way we used to, when time was young. We didn't have to talk, just smile. Each of us, although in our own thoughts, felt a connection through the same likings. Sameness is what connects us all!

Immortelle de Neige

Overnight, the flower in my soul bloomed. The warm rays of life finally reached through the far edges of the glacier where it lay dormant, encapsulated in ice. I could barely notice its floret, hidden among patches of limestone and snow. Lastly, I grew to be an *immortelle de neige*!

Loyalty

Sometimes it is nice to get away from materialities and rational abstractions and dwell in the intangible, butterfly-like world of *a priori* emotions. Without being prejudiced by either the physical reality or the mind, sentiments are truly elating and frank—a compass in life.

The Blissful Feminine

What a joy it is to play rapt in feelings and imaginings that come from a place of instinctual connectedness with all that exists! At long last, my soul settled to nest in the midst of the blissful feminine. Unexplored, a virgin and stunning realm awaits the awakening of humankind.

Preparing for Spring

Pregnant tree branches are glowing in the morning rays of sun. Oh, life is again at its dawn to enchant our being with the hope of new beginnings. I can see dreams budding again, alert and vivacious, hardly waiting to burst forth. Once more, the world will be filled with colors!

Following a Purpose

Each thread of white hair on my head is a poem that I wrote. It is my way of cocreating the life that flows through me, unavoidably—sometimes smoothly, sometimes gurgling loudly as it falls through hollows and ravines. Worth is found in our choice to age with a purpose in mind!

Recurrent

Another cycle had come again with its hurt. All of a sudden my eyes opened wide as I grasped its gain. Each period, with its pain, facilitates a moment of reflection into the gift of life and of living. It offers women the respite to recompose and fill their soul with gratefulness.

The Final Dot

I stopped writing all of a sudden, for since I cannot do something perfect, at least I should find a balance between how much effort I put forth before I declare a creation finished. Who is to decide when and if a work of art is complete? Well, place a final dot, just like that.

Persistent yet Passing

Some poems are like oak trees, majestic, enduring, all encompassing; others are like fireflies, ephemeral, then again light and playful. Each has its own beauty and purpose. Side by side, they show the true nature of life and art—persistent, yet passing all at once.

Accountability for One's Own Journey

We find nothing in everyday distractions, yet we hide behind them to avoid accountability for a worthwhile journey. Excuses, justifications, postponing are only momentary cover-up stories. One's heart will always know the truth. Now is the time to pursue all we envisioned!

Through Hardships

Every successful person failed before, even more so. Each failure pushed them onward, toward unearthing from the depths of their souls the unexpected! For that process of overcoming hardships polishes one's creative expression to a gemlike quality.

Hidden Toil

The flowers are always blooming without warning. The visible transformation from bud to blossom occurs abruptly, the same as birth—and the indiscernible shows its face. Yet the progression toward that point of emergence takes months of hidden groundwork.

The Sound of Life

Pic, pic, pic, the sky cries and sobs by my window. *Drip, drop, drop,* each grain of sand in the hourglass tumbles. *Thud-thud,* the heart beats. I am alive! My heart beats, *thud-thud.* Tumbles each grain of life in the hourglass. By my window, tears fall, *pic, pic, pic.* I am alive!

A Beautiful Realm

Let *a priori* dreams flow flamboyant and elating, loving and unintentional. Don't allow fear tame and box your imagination into a factual line of thought. The tangible reality is just the tip of the iceberg. Why give up to the joys of your intricate inner world, idealistic and pure?

The Freedom of Expression

I can contribute so much more to the world when I let myself manifest the way I am. I can give back so much less when I try to align my expression to outer pressures and expectations. I am childish and unpractical, and this is the value I bring forth. Nobody has to endorse it at all!

The Blessing in All Our Differences

Our differences are a blessing, for they bring color to the world and reverence to our interactions. In the middle of contrast, we find ourselves and learn where we fit. Our inner universe expands through every divergent point of view. Seeing all the facets of life makes us whole!

Ode to the Hidden Feminine

I bestow this poem to the hidden feminine nature in all human beings—to the kindness and sensitivity in us, to our sense of meekness in serving others, and to the idealistic part of our thoughts that help us believe in peace and love. May we all learn to free our feminine side!

Shared Beauty

Each one of us is a flower among flowers, each stunning, each bringing its own contribution to the world. Although beautiful in itself, from afar no one has preponderance over the other, but work together to bring out their shared glory in a vibrant field of color.

An Ode to Life

Death brings us together in ways nothing else can. Pain and grief become a shared bridge based on common trials. We bow our heads in reverence for what we have: a life! Weeping as one, our humanity opens up and blossoms like flowers in springtime.

Ode to Mary

Blessed are thee, mother of Incarnated God, for you accepted a burden that no other human did, wavering not even once. You endured the hurt seeing your Son die, lamenting not even once. You were indeed the portal to new life, yet you claimed accolades not even once!

The Language of Nature

Nature talks to us in a way nothing else can. "Hush, hush," it whooshes through leaves, "let worries go," and somehow we open up and release our tensions. "Be at peace," it murmurs by the water, and somehow our soul quiets down. Nature knows the language of the nature in us.

Find Your Passion

Friend, what is troubling your soul? Are there malignant cells and the physical pain that comes with it or the cancerous thoughts that shoves and hurls your spirit through endless torment? Find that one thread of passion that represents you, that begets joy even into the darkest days!

The Warmth of Spring

My bones are cold, not from the taciturn touch of winter, but rather from the impersonal and soundless vibe of closed rooms. The light stretches through the curtains. I jerk back. Slowly, my bones uncurl. I open the window and let spring come in. The warmth of life feels good!

The Consciousness Edifice

Several times in one's life, the portal into wondering of the purpose and worth of life opens. The metaphysical context of one's inner-consciousness edifice, with its cornerstone and basic principles, smashes to smithereens. We can build it back as it was, or fully change its structure.

The Wondering Portal

We awaken once in a while, at key moments of our life, and step through the wondering portal. The choice of what it is that gives meaning to our existence—seeds we select to plant—governs our pursuits, the fruits that we will harvest, and the glee we find in all that life is!

The Cornerstone of Love

Once more, I spotted the wondering portal. I stepped in, this time without apprehension. Seeing the ruins of my past consciousness did not sadden me, for I was ready to bury it and erect on a different ground, a totally new edifice. First, I placed east the Cornerstone of Love.

Young Human Souls

With a delicate and suave appearance and a fresh tone, the budding leaves spring on a contorted spiral, with an essential purpose for all life. It reminds me of young human souls coming into this world fresh, delicate, and suave, with an essential purpose in life!

Human Buds

In awe, I beam, witnessing how the miracle of life unfolds vivaciously each spring. The same, with warmth I smile at each young soul that sprouts on Earth, unique like each bud and meant to blossom. Through the fresh eyes of younglings, our culture and humanity flourishes!

Approximation of Approximation

It is hard to find the best expression of thoughts in words—my poems are just approximations. Actually, thoughts are approximations as well; approximations of inner and outer perceptions. Many times, the approximation of another approximation yields false utterances and notions!

An Ordered Disorder

Order and disorder coexist. Each impinges on the other to conquer the status quo of facts and events. As one settles in, the other one becomes peripheral. Amidst the joined struggle, change becomes possible. Freedom of expression is found in the moment of overturning.

A Disordered Order

Disorder and order coexist. Order finds a way to pattern the loose ends of disorder, and disorder, to scatter all that is configured in order. One builds on and escapes from the other at the same time, in an unpredictable predictability. And this is how the world transforms.

Unpredictable Predictability

We can never catch on to the truth because the transformations in reality, as they occur, are always a step ahead of our understanding of them. Although the world might evolve in predictable ways, all possible details and combinations render it unpredictable.

Predictable Unpredictability

Choice is unpredictable, yet man chooses in a predictable fashion not against his ways, but according to them. Once in a while, one breaks barriers with a lateral move. This change, although predictable, affects unpredictably the world, setting up the imprint for new norms.

Oppression against Oneself

Finally, I broke the shackles of my preconceptions and freed myself from my oppressive ruling. Not that I become unbiased all of a sudden, but that the bias toward myself does not control my actions anymore. I can be all that I want in spite of all that I am not!

Capriccio

The blissful feminine has unexplored depths. It is pure energy, free of shape. Travels beyond the speed of light or stays still in the moment, as it wishes, following the *capriccio* of *a priori* love. The world shines at its magical touch, like the warmth of spring that drives all flourishing.

The Hidden Muse

My muse ... I denied its existence. She was born to serve me and remained devoted. From the shadow of my ignorance, she reached always toward my feet to spark within me inspiration. I spotted her image one of those days in the mirror. She smiled—my muse ...

Nothing More and Nothing Less

I found myself just to get lost, blissfully, in my true universe. I am in between nothing more and nothing less, at peace. Without any pressure, nothing more and nothing less I can manifest in my life. Value and freedom lie in the process of regeneration itself.

The Primordial Assumption

The universe exists beyond us, yet what we understand about the universe cannot be but subjective, from the stand of one's primordial assumption in which all other truths stem. Change the cornerstone, and the consciousness edifice tumbles! The universe will still exist…

The Tree of Senses

A spirit cannot touch the petals of the cherry blossoms nor breathe in the freshness of spring… It is not from the tree of knowledge that Eve tasted, but from the tree of senses—an apple denied to all nonincarnated beings. And this is the singularity of a man's life!

Sacred Existence

Knowledge is a consequence of what comes through our internal and external senses—from *a priori* emotions and reveries, from all that the material world offers, the touching, the sounds, the smell... Oh, how ephemeral is our existence, yet how unbelievably blessed!

When Innocence Dies

The fruit appealed to Eve's youthful candor. *What if I touch it?* she wondered. The apple felt good in her hands. The apple had a fragrance like no other. "Bite," the snake held. "It tastes good as well!" For it contrived through the senses to deceive and conquer the soul of Man!

The Fall of Man

The Garden of Eden turned upside down. "Man ate from the tree—no one else did!" all heavenly beings roared, pulling their hair. "Man has to die; there is no turning back! He can know now what none of us can!" God hid the being who can feel on Earth, and vowed redemption on his behalf.

The Protector

God placed the Human in the physical realm, where neither good nor bad spirits can reach him; taught the youngling the laws of the new land, counseled him how to live in peace and thrive… Our life on Earth is under the wing of God. The fight to save our soul happens before we die.

The Divine Touch

Man did not listen to God's word. He presumed free will is enough to render him contentment in life. Relentlessly searching for a way to connect, God incarnated to appeal to Man's heart. He assumed all our pains and all our sins and died for us, so that we can live through him!

A Gifted Life

What sets Man apart from the animal kingdom is his ability to wonder with his mind and create with his hands. But what sets Man apart from the angelic realm is the gift of feeling the world around. After all, he lost his eternal life to gain this insight!

A Woman's Innocence

Since the beginning of the world, man kneels in the face of a young maid's innocence. He covets her virtue, yet as soon as she loses it, he turns a cold eye in disdain. What man forgets is that the true innocence of a prodigious woman is not in her body, but in her heart!

Most Favorable Outcome 1

The world does not need to function in predetermined patterns. Laws do not sustain the world—rather, the world optimizes itself, and its optimal functioning transfers to laws. As soon as a path of least resistance is found, the universe adjusts itself to new laws and patterns.

Most Favorable Outcome 2

Man has the freedom to choose behaviors less optimal for his own self. He can take a detour just to enjoy the view, or give a hand to someone in need just because it feels good. Man can choose to change one's ways at any moment because one's life is more than moving along mindlessly!

Hanging from Clouds

Sometimes the blissful feminine in me is tired and turns upside down, hanging from clouds. Dreams and hopes get a respite. In that moment of quietness, the meaning of life is escaping me once more. I am waiting to rain new beginnings over useless concerns…

The Inexistent Door

Searching with an open heart cannot lead anyone astray. Let the blissful feminine flow. Door after door will open wide; not because you found a key to unlock any, but that no gate was ever standing. The barriers you thought you saw are made of butterflies guiding you out!

Freedom in Beauty

I wish I understood life sooner. Knowing what one can and cannot expect from society at large, from any relationship, and from one's own self, is liberating. Once there, one can see and appreciate beauty in the confinement of imperfection.

Progressive Society

I am in a position in which I have freedom to reflect on the beauty of life. All modern societies should offer a peaceful and tolerant background to make the reflection on the beauty of life possible. Saddened, I know that so little of the world today has peaceful circumstances.

The Strength of Our Humanity

Everyone should have the freedom to learn how to manifest one's own blissful feminine without fear or restrictions. Since it is pure and humble inner-love and peacefulness, we should encourage and nurture it. The blissful feminine is the strength of our humanity, not its flaw.

The Impossible Equation

One pebble hitting still waters reverberates in perfect circles; more pebbles disturb the surface in an overlapping interference pattern. But men are not pebbles, and their deeds don't occur in still waters. No equation can contain the joint effect of factors set in motion by each action.

The Flower in Me

I am trying to discover in life the exact circumstances for the spark within me to ignite. I couldn't position myself just right yet, in a warm spot, in a fertile ground, for the flower in me to sprout and emerge into the light. Spring will eventually descend upon my heart!

Ever-Present Biases

We are all faulty of biases. What we need to build up is our tolerance for differences in biases—the understanding that a different stance comes with a different window into the world. Embracing different views raises man above his self-centered, limiting condition.

Responsibility

We focus too much on human rights and too little on human responsibilities. It takes nothing to demand deference. It counts notably to respect all life alike, to contribute to the well-being of the world and not take away from it, to provide, to yield, to assist, to be a Human Being!

Dew

Defying Gravity

The human being is nothing more than a pristine droplet hanging on a grass stalk. Defying gravity, it ascends toward a blade's tip as if to reach infinity. It gleams for a minute, touched by a ray of light. Live well that minute, human, find the spark in you!

The Embrace of Uncertainty

Life keeps me hanging from a thread above the abyss of incertitude. "Learn to balance," Life uttered, "or the drift will break and you will fall apart!" Giving up to worries did not modify my circumstances, but it helped me embrace the uncertainty of life. The world looks much brighter!

The Forgotten Feminine "I"

I walked in the shadow of "He" and "They," looking from distance at what made him, the "He," and them, those "They." It took me a lifetime to learn how to bring "I" forward. "I" love, "I" am important, "I" can succeed. Oh, how liberating and empowering this "I," in active voice, feels!

In the Middle

Life starts somewhere in the middle; not when one is born, but rather when one becomes aware. From that point, one moves forward and backward all at once, grasping the present while making sense of the past. Who am I from the multitude of possible descriptors, who am I?

Uncovering Life's Ethos

What we create is as distinctive as a fingerprint, intimately linked to our life's ethos. The more one uncovers that inner world, the more grandiose one's work of art grows. Through each new universe exposed, the knowledge and understanding of humanity expands as well.

Raising above Labels

I noticed being a girl mattered when labels boxed me in that particular corner. I understood class, race, age, to be advantaged or disadvantaged, when each was deemed relevant by the context. Each put pressure on my behavior and attitude, but none makes me who I am.

Reassessing Life's Lessons

She saw herself in the eyes of her pupils and had to revisit her own emergence through their hurdles. Her own struggle growing up became poignant and painful once more. Only this time, she was able to reassess the lessons of life with an open mind.

Life Lessons

How we parent, how we teach, how we interact with others is directly related to what we had or needed growing up. In the end, everything we do helps us understand who we are and where we stand. From all the havoc of figuring out life, some lessons we will pass down.

Visceral

Once in a while, a tremendous craving for the human touch overwhelms my being. Nothing can appease this longing, no personal belief, no other pursuit. We are not self-sufficient in life; we need another soul standing by our side, one's love, one's touch of all our physical insides.

Faceless Lover

In my reverie I see you, my faceless lover, holding me in your arms. In your arms, my walls melt, exposing the nakedness of my soul. As I accept your physical caressing, my mind opens up and lets the feelings manifest unshackled. I long for the love dream to become a reality!

My Lens

I did not walk but dance first, my mother said. My poetry is a dance of words; my paintings, a dance of colors... Dance is my lens—I see the world though the most imperceptible vibrations, through the interconnectivity of sway, through free-flowing love and self-willed expression.

From the Peak of the Mountain

Man is a poet deep inside, for he has awe to wonder into infinity and love to share one's heart. He has positioned himself on the peak he conquered through trials and pains—a place that earned him a vantage point. From there, he can show the world the beauty of new horizons!

A Drop of Dew

What lies further, further above, below, inside, beyond life, beyond the end of the end? Man is a troubadour through his limited existence, limited from above, below, inside, before his life, before the beginning of the beginning. Man finds a drop of dew sparkling in the morning sun.

Moment of Awareness

Man finds a drop of dew sparkling in the morning sun. And in that drop he sees reflected the sky above, the Earth below, and his own wondering eyes. For a moment, he exists in that drop and is the drop of dew sparkling in the morning sun—a miracle of life!

Knock Knock

This is our measuring tool, the palm of our hand. We see and know what we can reach and touch. But, if we hold hands together, our understanding expands beyond our life to tap into different spaces and cultures. Our widening humanity knocks on the door of our hearts!

The Beautiful Being You Are

She always passed by, always ignoring herself, her needs and dreams... she felt so irrelevant. After her youth and raising children befell, after she left behind all societal discourses about what should represent one's life, she saw herself for the first time—a beautiful being!

Societal Preconceptions

Societal discourses impinge a person into believing life should follow a certain course, after certain rules and aims. Spread to control people's thoughts and actions, they are meant to simply provide direction—as a guideline, not an absolute. Free yourself of preconceptions!

The Creative Mien

Some people show their creativity though an original style or a new way of expression; others further what was done before them or what was not concluded; some bring different lenses to the table, and some different angles. All have the same resolution: to build awareness.

A Window into the Unknown

Art is a window into the unknown. It shows people what they did not see before, on their own. The more it elicits thoughts and feelings in another, the more valuable is the work, with a life of its own—a creation that creates. From a tiny seed, a majestic tree will grow into infinity!

Creative Mode of Being

I am a creator. It is my nature, my mode of being, of loving, of living. I create, and through my expression I am being created. Creating builds me. Art is the way I share my heart, connect, discover, learn, transcend to new realms... Above, the blue open sky is smiling!

The Magical World of Imagination

She finds refuge in the swirly lines she draws over and over and over till the shapes absorb her into a magical world of imagination. Her creative state is an inward implosion—a place in which she redefines herself again and again. Art is for her more than an escape; it is a transcendence!

The Path of Butterflies

I don't run from reality through art, but rather construct it the way I see and experience it. I don't hide my emotions in art, but rather let them dance freely. I never know on what path the butterflies are taking me. I know it always leads into a meadow, full of flowers and light!

Awaken!

People choose the undisturbed oblivion in the comfort of their homes. Their mind is asleep and their feelings numbed. Yes, awareness comes with hurt for the pain that exists in the world. Taking action becomes unavoidable. Awaken, the priceless act of giving a hand costs nothing!

The Tower of Babel

How we built our individual reality and collectively manage our society cannot sustain humanity anymore. The Tower of Babel crumbles, for we are failing to find the language that unites us—care for each other and for all life. Awaken, the priceless act of giving a hand costs nothing!

A Sense of Alienation

Alienation grows strong within me at times. All meanings crumble. I find myself alone, carrying a dense, powerlessness feeling. I want to run, but there is nowhere to hide from a feeling. Through years of disillusions, I learned that separation is as much part of life as togetherness is!

In Our Own Skin

We are always alone, separated by the limits of our skin. We see what we see and bear our own feelings… To hear another, to endure another, is a choice. Togetherness requires effort and dedication. Without it we cannot but be alone, separated by the limits of our ego.

Lost in the Life's Waves

Oh, how alone a youngster feels, as if the world conspires against him. He struggles to find himself and his place while making sense of life's realities. Most will try hard and learn from their toils and angsts how to stay afloat, but a few will get lost in the rip current.

The Other Side

Men toss belittling words as acid in a woman's face, trying to make ugly that which they cannot handle to see independent. Women walk forward, hurt but not broken, suffering but not giving up—for in spite of a callous portrayal of them, they know how and who they are!

The Cover-Up

If the man is not the powerful one, then what remains of him? A timid soul, insecure and frightened, so dependent on a kindred soul's support, like a child. Like a child, he covers up his weaknesses with a mask of hegemony and pretends to be in control!

Strength of Character

So many have a calling, yet so few answer it. Even less choose to fight through life's adversities. The ones who push forward against the current end up being the Titans of humankind. We honor their talent, but what truly stands out is their strength of character!

The Treasures of the Soul

I either die or I live—I told myself one day—let the world inside me vanish, or help it flourish. Since then, I wander through the endless beauties of my soul. From time to time, I bring tiny treasures into being, the same as the ocean's waves drop shells from its deeps onto the shore.

On a Gust of Wind

"Where are you taking me?" "The world over, or rather, the life," the wind said, "into heights and depths and insides, into blues and springs, over snow, over oceans…" "Why?" I asked. "Who cares?" the gust answered. "Without the free dance in the wind, life is nothing!"

On a Stream of Water

"Where are you taking me?" "To the spring of life," the water answered, "digging a path though hardships, restlessly, ceaselessly, unwinding, stretching to new limits…" "Why?" I asked. "Who cares?" the river countered. "Move on, push on—standing still helplessly solves nothing."

In the Cracking of Flames

"It burns, it hurts, let me go!" "No way," the fire replied. "You cannot stop your heart's fervor. Let it burn, let it consume you... Manifest what you are!" "Why?" I asked. "Who cares?" the flames retorted. "Since you are alive, you might as well live with fiery passion!"

Walking the Earth

Only the dirt on which I walk is silent, for it knows I will return to it one day. Some things in life are inescapable. But since one breathes, one might as well shine, express, embrace life with all that is inescapable, experience love in all its forms…

The Voice of Circumstances

Some emotions I never show, I think. Some facts do not affect me, I think. But once in a while a melody of sorrow, and pain, and grief resonates in my heart. We are a product of our circumstances as much as we are of our own dreaming!

Following Ezio Bosso

"I am not scared," he shouted, while his terminal illness disabled his body each day more profoundly. "I will follow a bird," he hummed, with my mind on the (re)wind. "I can push through this sweet and bitter taste of life, with thunders and lightning. I live between trees and clouds!"

Sorting through Cares

I don't care anymore. I really don't, "don't care," but by not caring about irrelevant matters, I made space to focus on what I do care about. It is an imperative life process to sort through cares till you find the ones without which your identity and exuberance die out!

The Weight That Holds Dreams Down

Some cares are not worth caring about. Like flying a dirigible on a collision course, I had to relinquish weight over weight to stay afloat. So little I need to sail—dreams in the wind, strength to stir and push forward, and love to touch other's lives through my journey.

The Enchanted Bird of Light

She was wandering blindly through a forsaken land. All pushed her away, full of spite, for they could not bear to see a soul beautiful beyond measure. The Enchanted Bird of Light descended from Heavens and spit on her lids. "Open your eyes, child, creation is yours to master!"

The Glee of the Present Moment

I am not searching anymore for a happiness that stands grand and tall in a faraway future I might never get to know. I stare at each moment instead to see what lies within—a drop of dew, a flower that just bloomed, the sky's blue. Glee rests in the simple things around us!

The Stars Above, the Stars Within

When all the human lights are out, the stars shine bright in darkness. The same, when all distractions man sets aside, his awareness revives. And as the light of stars dispels without one noticing its uniqueness, one's awareness dies too, as if it never existed.

Up to You

How the wind blows, how the rain falls, how barriers raise, how relationships shift, how society dictates, nobody can fully control. But how Man uses the wind, how he manages the rain, how he pushes through jams, how he builds relationships, how he attunes to society—is up to Him!

A Spirit Untamed

I take in my hand what I can control and let anger and remorse burn for what I cannot. My hesitant stance stood against me more so than any life hardships. As I remove each layer of apprehension, my spirit grows untamed, instinctively following its natural stream.

Just Storms Passing By

Clouds come and leave on airstreams. Storms also form, with thunder and lightning; consume their amassed energy with force but break down and dissipate swiftly. Yet man holds clouds and storms over his head long after they passed by completely!

Mother Nature's Lessons

Be a rock that stands tall amidst winds and storms. Be the river that continues its flow around barriers. Be a sapling, bending but not breaking, rooted on solid ground. Learn from nature how to endure yet still grow, push through, manifest your true call.

Life's Caprices

Clouds and storms come and go—caprices of life. Nothing more than what they appear to be—clouds and storms rustling through—caprices are acrid and bossy, but brief. One can hold its gloom over one's head or let them go as fast as they came—to caprices, either way is the same.

A Patch of Blue

She held onto the clouds—hard to say why. Perhaps she did not know how to let go. She held onto the clouds for so long till the gloom, the gray, the lack of horizon became prevalent. How can a spirit escape such confinement? By opening up a patch of blue, one at a time!

Regardless of the Drift of Clouds

I had a bad habit, while young, of gathering dark clouds over my head. Many were not even mine; some were stray; some were nonsensical… After years and years of misery, I opened my hand. The glumness scattered. I learned to mind my path regardless of the drift of clouds.

Stumbling upon a New Frontier

Oh, little bird, you ventured beyond your known territory into a new frontier where your eyes cannot distinguish a way through among barriers. Worried, I witness your trials, yet I know it is up to you to find an open window. A similar struggle endures an artist.

Unchanged Blue

What happened? The sky is still blue and I carry within the same unbound innocence. Yet the splendor of my facade is gone in the wind. I swallow sorrowful bitterness. Like all younglings, I did not know what I had. The sky is still blue, unchanged…

A Few Seeds Left to Plant

I want to cry once in a while for the dreams of my childhood I let go without pursuing. I want to wail once in a while for the passion of my youth I unleashed fruitless. Instead, I will seize the moment of today, and full of gratitude, seed the dreams and passion I have left.

Whimsical Reminiscence

A song from the past bled through the present, full of nostalgia. I don't know if I should be joyful or sad reminiscing over its poetry and romance. "Go back," I say. "Go back to your time!" But the song continues its joyful and sad refrain. Poetry and romance are both part of life!

What Life Has to Offer

At times, when I see a youthful look, I wish to be the same once more. Sighing, I remember that the wheel of time turns as fast, as unforgiving for everyone, and that the starting point makes no difference. What I had is all that life offers—some trials, some pain, some joy, some love…

Degrees of Freedom

Man dwells in limbo, between an utterly objective and an utterly subjective certainty. Both are in continual change, as it is man's perception of them. The number of degrees of freedom one finds in a system full of constraints determines one's life direction and magnitude.

The Subjective-Objective Interface

The water imitates itself. When a pebble reaches it, the ripples are determined by both, the water's properties as impacted by the ones of the rock. The same, one's subjectivity is moved by manifold facets of objective reality. The aftermath is a result of their interface.

Sifting through Grains of Sand

Some things that one sees don't exist; some that exist, one doesn't see. And here is a man's dilemma: what is purely objective from what is purely subjective in all that he feels, in all that he thinks? In incertitude, he vacillates, sifting through grains of sand for the truth's mark.

A Flower's Purpose

I am writing because I have something to say. Through writing, I exist. I guess this is the search in one's life—for existence—moments in which one expresses what one is meant to. Like a flower head, one shows the world one's very essence. Each one of us aspires to bloom!

Like a Dewdrop

This is how man comes into existence: like dew, through a set of favorable conditions. The droplet holds together in its skin; no different, man stays whole, fighting forces that pull him apart. When the time comes, man vanishes from Earth, the same as the dew after sunrise.

An Accolade

My son got me a flower, not to remind me of my beauty that passed as fast as a blossom, but rather for me to see and acknowledge the beauty I inspired in his heart. Spring after spring, flowers will blossom. Beauty persists through the buds that come after us!

A New Page

A New Page

This is a new page, free of expectations. I cannot visualize where the road will lead me. All that I see is an opening in the unrevealed, a little light calling warmly, softly. For the first time in my life, I don't doubt its chime. With poise, I step into the unknown, for I have a message to deliver!

The Master Builder

Whatever I built by day crumbled by night. I couldn't sift the true calling from all the interfering sounds. I had to reach bottom in order to free the enchanted bird of light in me. I had to make the ultimate sacrifice—give up everything in order to find the one thing that really mattered.

What Can You Do Today?

Do. Do. Do whatever crosses your mind. Start and finish. This is what makes life—each moment lived fully, with passion, loving someone or something, exploring, discovering... Ask yourself, "What else can I do today that makes me happy?" Invent the worthwhile of each pursuit!

Lessons for the Future

What lessons of the past hold true? When to plow the field, how to navigate the sea, whom to trust in our path—count in a positive way. Yet winds change, the grounds shift, people come and go, and lessons of the past might not hold true. Sift through knowledge, but build all skills!

In New Light

If we conjure the past, thoughts and emotions, good and bad, distorted memories of distorted perceptions flood the present moment. Yet once in a while, we should bring them out of the closet, reexamine situations in a new light, and reassess what makes us who we are.

A Mourning Process

The past, good and bad, is in us, with us; real and imagined experiences influence our view, our reactions, our hopes for the future. Any hurt, like a mourning process, takes time to heal, takes crying and lamentation. Without mourning, wounds will continue to bleed…

A Resolve to an Unresolved Past

I do not know how to mourn my hurt. I get stuck between feeling a loss and reexperiencing it over and over and over with the same intensity. Somehow, I cannot discern or adopt a resolve to what is already permanent. A huge tail of unsettled issues slows down my progress.

The Hinge

Every man is setting the course for the path that one is to follow. It starts beyond a dream, with the decision "I want to …" and continues with a step in front of the other, day after day. Success does not hinge on favorable circumstances as much as it does on one's determination.

Farewell, Regrets of the Past, Farewell

The time has come to forgive myself for all that I was not, for all that I did not. As I toss each regret one by one into the fire, I thank all that befell and say a proper farewell. As I toss each regret one by one into the fire, I make space in my heart for new joys and pursuits.

Affirmation

I affirm: "The past does not have a hold on me anymore!" I affirm: "I am breaking free of destructive patterns of thought." I affirm: "I Am, and by Being, I want to manifest my existence the way I find it fit." Barriers won't stop me, for I have learned how to rise above!

Imprinted Message

The message is essential in true art. What it is that the artist chooses to share with the world, what emotion, state, idea, principle? To materialize the intention is up to one's toil. Like a fern, the creation unfurls into the future on a spiral, replicating the message in each detail.

Trickles of Water

"I have many ideas in my head," she said. "I need to spill them out, or else they build mental pressure and render me useless!" No matter the reason for expression, an artist cannot live without it. Through the creative flow their life grows—each trickle of water merges into a river.

The Gift of Awareness

We are of the universe, for it had pulled all forces together to make our becoming possible. The universe is of us, for only we can acknowledge its existence. Vicariously, we live through each other. The universe has eternity on its side; while us, an infinitesimal moment of sentience!

Lunation Effect

Every so often, a lunation cycle disturbs my daily ruminations with immense strength. Contrary to expectations, the disturbance comes from a total quiet down of inner waters—a void of thought and emotions, as if life had come to a halt. Patiently, I wait for the waves to return.

Unpausing

Summertime passes, irrespective of doings and not doings. Hot and lazy is all there is. Storm surges bring some relief. It takes over the hot and lazy daze for a minute. Yet I want nothing more than for those days to stay forever as they are—hot and lazy.

Spiritual Fungi

We do not need to go through the same experience to relate to the pain of another. Everyone can find in one's repertoire of aches and troubles something of a similar struggle. Hidden to the naked eye, there is a network of spiritual fungi that keeps all of us connected.

Ground for a Much Better Future

Teach young minds how to grow forever young, not with custom ways of thinking, but with the freedom and strength to envision what nobody else could, to stretch to lengths nobody else reached. Create a base not just for the good you know, but for much better!

Uphill

What do you want to remember from life? Success, everyone wants to summon up, but to reach success, no matter how one defines it, one needs to go through setbacks and errors and the pain that comes with them. The road to achievement is filled with failed trials!

A Doubtful Base of Thought

One principle, one idea, one assumption has to lie at the center of anyone's inner world. Everything else gravitates around it, closer to the core or remote, toward the outskirts of any logic. However, that one fundamental assumption is based on uncritical thought.

A Helping Hand from the Beyond

We climb the ladder of human tenets till we reach the limit of our incompetency. There, without a horizon to strive toward, we hang out in complete and utter disappointment. All of life seems trite from the top of the pyramid. From the top, only the beyond can help us!

Infallible Richness

I am wondering why we value so much thinking as if it is what makes us human, as if we depend on it, as if it is our infallible richness toward a better life. I feel that the heart is what makes us Human, on which our sparkle depends, our infallible richness toward a better life!

Unshackled Ways of Thinking

Think. Who is to say how to think? Since when did it become a predetermined exercise, part of a lesson plan? Let the spirit of children learn freely how to search and discover their own zeniths, for they do not live for today, but for a tomorrow that nobody knows!

A Ray of Light

I teach not because of what I know, but because of what I want to learn! I witness the world being built again and again in the hope that one day, something will click and a change will occur in the souls of the young—souls that are to uplift us all to new realms!

Life's Territory

Nothing new about the pain I feel. I found no strategy to quell it. Perhaps it comes with life, like a packet—you get everything it entitles without knowing if you can or cannot endure all. I shall accept this pain, as it stems from the same sensitivity that allows me to enjoy being.

Hidden Breaking Point

Pulled down by the fruits, under its own weight, the branches of the peach tree sheared off. One should bear only enough yields to be able to pull through the summer storms unshattered. But how is it for one to know where the breaking point lies of one's soul?

Fruitful Souls

And the bees harvest its nectar, and the birds peck on it, and the squirrels hustle to bury the peaches somewhere into the ground, a place known just by them. All living nourishes off the fruitful tree. The same, communities flourish through bountiful souls!

Unconsoled

It thunders and lightnings up close, forcefully. The rain downpours so heavily, as if the sky is having a total mental breakdown. It cries and it weeps, it moans and it howls from one side of the horizon to the other. And perhaps, unconsoled, it is our pain befalling into the gray…

From Nexus to Nexus

Our spiritual expansion cannot be contained. Our inner galaxies move away from each other to uncharted territories. Our thoughts wander from nexus to nexus to find and give meaning to life. It is, however, the vast void in between that overwhelms us.

Counterintuitive

A new page we turn. Yet we write the same content over and over again. Chained to old habits that impede our growth, edgily, we seek change. Every time we strain, we sink deeper into quicksand. The startling move is to trust, look up at the sky, and let oneself fall backward.

Different Lenses

A new page we turn, or so we wish. We do not know how to paint the novel, for we look at the world through the same lenses, with the same colors, the same words, the same sense… The change has to occur in the heart, through a softness that we have to let be!

I Was—I Am

The old pages of my book of life, like leaves, are plunging further and further into the abyss of time. Full of nostalgia, I witness as they dance on a gust of wind. I cannot but smile—I was, I lived, I loved. I still am, I live, I love, and I write a new page...

Open Up to Much More

We build on our past feelings, thoughts, and experiences, but they don't bind us; we can choose to act according or in spite of them, following what they taught us or trying a new path. What shall one pick—to trust what one knows, or to trust that life can give one so much more?

Untried Paths

We can definitely get lost in the real world, but in the mind, no matter what path we take, it is still part of us. Although we can go wherever we want, we choose the familiar routes. As such, we miss the opportunity to discover all the wonders of our zeniths and our depths!

Toward the Natural State

To breathe and walk on Earth, the flesh ascends, the soul descends, and both unite into a human being. One part suffers the other's downside till the point at which each yearns to return to their natural state—one pulls toward the dirt, the other, toward the azures…

As a Short End of the Stick

As I age and fall physically weary, spiritually, I expand freer and freer of any worldly concerns. Feeble I grow in the flesh, but my soul ascends hearty and buoyant. What a fate is given to life—to always be extraordinary in some ways and inadequate in others!

An Extraordinary Life

How can it be to live such a dreary life, yet feel each trite moment so vibrantly? It is as if I embark on an adventure after an adventure, forever fit and ready to conquer the world. The wind blows just right in my sail, and the stars themselves are guiding my way!

Where the Value Lies

The value of my art does not lie in its sophistication, but rather its simplicity of expression; not in the shrewdness of ideas, but rather in the innocence of the search; not in telling the truth, but rather in the truthfulness of the telling—the beauty of a butterfly meandering friskily…

Limitless

We know little about ourselves, sometimes much less than we know about the surrounding world. It takes a lot of toil to become aware of our own constraints, and more so, about our expansion possibilities. There is no end to it and yet, we let ourselves be defined by limitations.

Gambling on Oneself

"I am getting there," she said. "To the realization that it is just me and myself facing life and infinity, to the realization that only I alone can make a difference in my days." On the edge of gambles, she is about to jump and embrace lovingly her own self!

Late Becoming

Women are beautiful like flowers when young, but they actually bloom late in life, between having their offspring leaving the nest and being blessed with grandchildren—a time when they try to figure out what to do with themselves and finally listen to the calling they always had!

The Eagerness to Learn

If you have a hunch, pursue it. Risk to make a fool of yourself rather than be a fool for not trying. The beauty of life stands in the challenges of a quest, not in the comfort of an established footing. The eagerness to learn is what pushes one to new summits.

With the Tides

What makes the tides of inspiration rise and fall? Is it the wind or a simple whim? The currents, or is it the will? Although distant, the moon seems to have a hand in it too, together with the tempests of life falling down upon us with questions and turmoil!

As a Reverberation

Inspiration can come as a reverberation, afterthoughts and after feelings following an ardent conversation, a stirring line in a book, an observation of nature's wonders, a reflective inquiry into life as a concept and our life as we face it. Yet one needs to be set to seize inspiration!

Following Butterflies

Inspiration is a butterfly that flutters freely, coming as if from nowhere and going as if it were never there. For a mere moment, it enchants our being with a fragrance hard to capture in a frame. For a mere moment, it sweeps us off our feet in a dreamy transcendence …

Uncharted Territory

One can notice how the water course from a mountain spring influences life down below, all the way toward its estuary and the sea. But there is another realm, an uncharted territory of unseen influences to which the course of our own thoughts and feelings must play a role!

Through a Dense Mist

If man imagined it, then it exists. The proof does not lie in finding any sort of concrete evidence; the proof is the feeling-thought itself. We might not have a way to name, describe, or grasp that which our intuition tells us exists. We perceive the undefined through a dense mist.

Encrypted Hint

When a feeling flows, a thought would follow closely, and when a thought ignites, in its shadow a feeling would emerge. Intuition is something in between—a kind of feeling-thinking about what is unseen, an awareness of the undefined, an encrypted hint from the beyond…

What If God Exists?

If God does not exist, I will lose nothing. For I seek piety, forbearance, and love regardless—it is how I choose to live my life, who to identify with, what to aspire toward… I live in God's shadow, not for the promise of a heavenly tomorrow, but for the majesty it gives to each day!

Invisible Helping Hand

The more you open to the possibility that a world beyond what is seen exists, the more you discern how that world is trying to shield you from harm, to guide you through obstacles and hardships, to aid you to find yourself and embark on the path to fulfill your life's mission.

Rising above Frailties

I went nowhere as long as I chose to depend on other people, hoping they would open the doors for my success. Now I walk slowly but on my own feet, toward my soul's zenith. Each step I take is a story of attainment—a triumph over my own frailties and drawbacks.

Semantics

I don't know in what language I think anymore. No way of expression has preeminence over another—and perhaps this is what it means to be truly multilingual. Instead of words, I think in colors and in feelings. After all, love and kindness are measured in smiles and geniality!

Knowing without Words

Although newborns have not experienced life yet and cannot distinguish forms clearly, they dream vividly as if they know something from before life, as if they are born with preknowledge. This preknowledge does not come as words or from words.

A Sense That Stands above Words

We have a sixth sense that stands above words. It comes in the form of intuition, creativity, and nonverbal communication. Yet our society is based on words, emphasizes words, teaches our young through words, and judges the universe, inner and outer, using words.

The Confinement of Words

Sometimes thinking in words slows us down; sometimes it limits our power of expression and growth. Sometimes breakthroughs come to us wordlessly. Liberated from the confinement of learned words and meanings, all of a sudden we can see new, unthought-of paths.

Wordless Creative Wave

"I need passion to create," she said, the artist. "Without passion, I am dead inside! All that I can do is copy myself. Inspiration comes to me as a tumultuous outpour of images. When the creative wave hits me, my hand feels the impulse to pin ideas down on canvas."

Tabula Rasa

A new page looks blank, but since the beginning of the universe—if there was a beginning—it is never entirely so, it is never completely blank, completely new as if spawned from nihility. But for Man, a new page means to make a change that opens one's soul to new possibilities.

Fragments of Truths

A flower not yet in bloom is not less of a flower. An idea that did not spawn from evidence as we think of it is not necessarily untrue. The patterns we observe are outer manifestations of a hidden "why"—and those just a fragment from a bigger picture. The truth stands on its own.

A Longing for Serenity

Sometimes it is hard to hear your own inner song in all the cacophony of juxtaposed, outer hums. I hear trumpets and drums, each following a separate tune. In times like this I long to be in the woods, where every sound adds to a feeling of oneness and harmony.

Pages Worth Remembering

Every new page we turn becomes old. Important is what we fill it with. Some pages are left as a barren scenery—nothing to remember but emptiness. But for others, we work diligently toward a goal—the landscape transforms in a wonder of our world.

A New Page

Oh, the page is complete. I am at the end of a story. Regretful I am to let go of what I grew fond of. But full of joyfulness I am as well for the new page, the new adventure I am about to embark on. My days are numbered, but how well I live each is of my doing!

About the Author

Cleopatra Sorina Iliescu was born in Transylvania in the beautiful city of Brasov, a medieval-looking urban area surrounded by majestic mountains. She lived her childhood and youth under the oppression of the harshest communist regime in Europe, which impeded to a high degree her life opportunities and suppressed her expression as a poet, writer, and visual artist. Although she managed to publish in Romania a few poems and short stories and participated in group exhibits, her artistic tries and trials were mostly hidden from the public eye.

She immigrated to the United States in her early thirties, already holding a degree in engineering and one in psychology. She continued her studies in Virginia, and graduated with a masters of science in applied psychology. Currently she works in a suburb of Atlanta as a high school teacher in the public-school system and is pursuing her doctorate in education at Kennesaw State University. She lives a simple life tending to her two sons, Emanuel and David, and their dog, Alida.

Throughout the years, she has continued in private her call and passion for the arts. Her first volume of verses, *The Blue Key*, with poems in the Romanian language gathered from her youth, was published in 2002. Her second volume of poetry, bilingual this time, *In the Shadow of a Rainbow*, followed in 2008. *An Angel with a Broken Wing* is her third book to be published, with three others in the works.